Cambridge Ele

Elements in Business Strategy
edited by
J.-C. Spender
Kozminski University

STRATEGIZING AI IN BUSINESS AND EDUCATION

Emerging Technologies and Business Strategy

Aleksandra Przegalinska
Kozminski University

Dariusz Jemielniak
Kozminski University

Shaftesbury Road, Cambridge CB2 8EA, United Kingdom

One Liberty Plaza, 20th Floor, New York, NY 10006, USA

477 Williamstown Road, Port Melbourne, VIC 3207, Australia

314–321, 3rd Floor, Plot 3, Splendor Forum, Jasola District Centre,
New Delhi – 110025, India

103 Penang Road, #05–06/07, Visioncrest Commercial, Singapore 238467

Cambridge University Press is part of Cambridge University Press & Assessment,
a department of the University of Cambridge.

We share the University's mission to contribute to society through the pursuit of
education, learning and research at the highest international levels of excellence.

www.cambridge.org
Information on this title: www.cambridge.org/9781009243551

DOI: 10.1017/9781009243520

First published 2023

A catalogue record for this publication is available from the British Library.

ISBN 978-1-009-24355-1 Paperback
ISSN 2515-0693 (online)
ISSN 2515-0685 (print)

Cambridge University Press & Assessment has no responsibility for the persistence
or accuracy of URLs for external or third-party internet websites referred to in this
publication and does not guarantee that any content on such websites is, or will
remain, accurate or appropriate.

Strategizing AI in Business and Education

Emerging Technologies and Business Strategy

Elements in Business Strategy

DOI: 10.1017/9781009243520
First published online: March 2023

Aleksandra Przegalinska
Kozminski University

Dariusz JemielniakHarvard University
Kozminski University

Author for correspondence: Aleksandra Przegalinska

Abstract: We propose a clear and up-to-date description of the state of artificial intelligence today, not only in terms of business processes and strategies, but also its societal reception. This Element presents our view of the technology landscape, avoiding both the forward-looking, rose-colored utopia and the hyper-apocalyptic gloom. It does so in a concise form, addressing a complex issue in nine concise and easy-to-read sections. Our aim is to discuss the current state of machine learning and AI in strategic management, and to describe the emerging technologies. We conceptualize their adoption, and then consider the effects of AI technologies' maturity in business organizations.

This Element also has a video abstract: www.cambridge.org/Strategizing AI in Business and Education_ Jemielniak/przegalinska_abstract

Keywords: AI strategy, artificial Intelligence in business, machine learning, generative AI, cognitive technologies

ISBNs: 9781009243551 (PB), 9781009243520 (OC)
ISSNs: 2515-0693 (online), 2515-0685 (print)

Contents

1 Introduction

We propose a clear and up-to-date description of the state of artificial intelligence (AI) today, not only in terms of business processes and strategies, but also its societal reception. This Element presents our view of the technology landscape, avoiding both the forward-looking, rose-colored utopia and the hyper-apocalyptic gloom. It does so in a concise form, addressing a complex issue in nine concise and easy-to-read sections.

Our aim is to discuss the current state of machine learning and AI in strategic management, and to describe the emerging technologies. We conceptualize their adoption, and then consider the effects of AI technologies' maturity in business organizations.

Most observers of the adoption of AI over the past decade would probably agree that AI hype is at its peak. Nearly half the self-described "AI companies" actually have little to do with AI (Olson 2019), and they are simply riding the coattails of the frenzy. Management gurus preach the incorporation of AI into organizational strategies lest the business risk imminent doom. In such an atmosphere, it is difficult to discern the value of AI and data science in mainstream business, without either underestimating or overestimating its possibilities. It is even harder to know how and where to introduce these technologies, so that they actually improve our strategy rather than amplify the noise.

Our Element fills this gap. We summarize where AI and data science state-of-the-art stand in business organizations, and how AI is a key component of the digital transformation. We also peek into the future to identify the likely pitfalls of AI misuse and challenges, and then discuss the probable development of AI strategies.

Equally importantly, we believe that our approach is distinctive in that we are looking at the potential future of AI through the lenses of collaboration, accessibility, openness, and democratization. We have chosen a similar perspective in our previous book, *Collaborative Society* (Jemielniak and Przegalińska 2020) and in this Element we explore AI's business applications, including the potential that collaboration offers. What we can say is that the greater accessibility of AI is already palpable, but volatile: AI is suspended between technological oligopoly where the use of black-boxed AI models is encouraged, and attempts to keep the algorithms as open as possible. AI as a discipline has been under increased pressure for trustworthiness and democratization (Burkhardt 2019; Luce 2019), while the more worrying aspects of no-code, easy-access AI – like deepfakes – started to emerge. We are trying to capture the early signals of a shift to open AI that relies on collaboration and

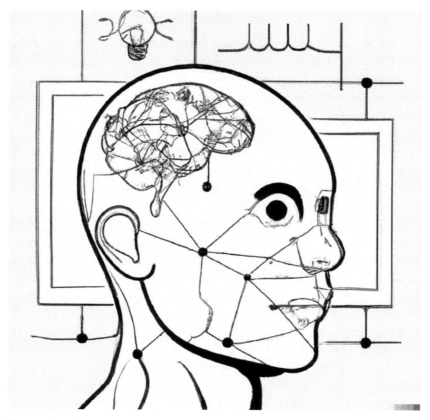

Figure 1 A picture generated by OpenAI's DALL·E 2 algorithm on 2022-10-29 with a prompt: "A black-and-white picture of artificial intelligence in business."

permeates almost all sectors of the economy while transforming business strategies and modes of working.

Finally, we use AI to enhance this Element in the belief that doing research, creating and analyzing spreadsheets, or writing with AI will become a state-of-the-art practice in the coming years. We begin each section with its summary generated by OpenAI "TL;DR" mechanism. Here and there, we have parts of sections written by fine-tuned GPT-3, OpenAI's large-scale language-generation model. In all cases, upon generating draft language, we reviewed, edited, and revised the language to our own liking and take ultimate responsibility for the content. In some (but not all) we highlight the verbatim excerpts. In the final section, we describe our collaboration with GPT, including all of its pitfalls, advantages, and challenges (Floridi and Chiriatti 2020).

First, in Section 2 we focus on the current state of machine learning, deep learning, and AI. The AI boom reached its next phase around 2018: implementation and reality check. A couple of years ago, discourse around AI mainly focused on possible future perspectives and a great deal of speculation. Artificial intelligence has already been implemented in agriculture, the legal field, retail, finance, education, and healthcare. The theme of this section is that AI will soon be used in all industries and businesses, and understanding its premises can go a long way in strategy.

In Section 3, we address the increasing problem of Fake AI (Kaltheuner 2021; Ruggeri et al. 2021): companies that ostensibly rely on AI but do not use AI technologies at all. We discuss the reasons for and the dangers of this practice. AI is such a popular technology that many companies abuse the term in their marketing to attract investors. We comment on this phenomenon and provide some guidelines on how to read between the lines.

In Section 4, we discuss the polarized perceptions of AI. We show that neither the doomsday Terminator-like scenarios nor the rose-colored utopias are particularly useful in understanding the ongoing revolution.

In Section 5, we discuss finding the proper place for AI in business strategy. Here, we answer the burning question of how organizations can start implementing AI. We present the key areas, leverage the biggest competitive advantage, and suggest a possible path that is based on extending existing business intelligence processes.

In Section 6, we revisit Porter's classic model of business strategies. Many experts claim that there are only two ways to compete: through cost leadership and premium. As Porter suggested, we can add focus, understood as orientation to clearly defined groups of users and customers. Artificial intelligence, however, combined with other technologies such as edge computing, may transform business strategies as we know them. We show that focus may become the dominant strategy. Companies that incorporate AI into their business processes are transforming not only their own operations, but their entire sector. Others, who decide to join this next level of digital and cognitive transformation, may indeed join too late. Laggers and experimenters who stop at the level of introducing one or two inconclusive pilot projects will not take AI to scale and reap its benefits. Yet, the pioneers are risking enormous resources for uncertain gains.

Section 7 is a study of transformers (i.e., foundational language models), and their place in business generally, and especially in marketing. We elaborate on the business applications of natural language processing and understanding (NLP and NLU, respectively) that deal with the interactions between computers and human language. The goal of NLP and NLU is to create a system capable of contextually "understanding" the content of documents, including the nuances of the language in them, and to converse freely with humans. As our case study in this section, we will use cutting-edge NLP tools such as transformer-based text generators like GPT-3, GPT-J, BERT or Bard.

Moving into the near future of AI, in Section 8 we focus on the "coopetitive" phenomenon (Le Roy and Fernandez 2015; Pellegrin-Boucher, Le Roy, and Gurău 2013). On the one hand, unique data sets and the first-mover's advantage are more important than ever; on the other hand, cooperating with direct competition is often the fastest way to secure them. Moreover, advances in AI technology are also relying on open-source models, which gives small players an unprecedented competitive advantage over larger players. In this section, we discuss the long-term consequences of "coopetition" for business strategies.

Section 9 makes a distinction between accessibility of AI (Wang et al. 2019) and its democratization. Artificial intelligence is not only becoming an increasingly complex and robust discipline but is also undergoing specialization and simplification. Many techniques, such as NLP, can be implemented without coding. We are going to focus on the low-hanging fruit from the point of view of organizational strategy and technological development, and suggest practical ways of building AI muscle. In the future, however, we will be thinking about AI as we are now thinking about the Internet. It is ubiquitous and it is obvious. No one treats it as a competitive advantage, and the playing field is leveled. We are also going to discuss the timeline and the ways, as well as the widespread application of AI, which will doubtlessly affect the way people work. In this section, we explore synergies between human workers and AI in managerial tasks, assuming that the future does not belong to automation of work, but rather to humans and AI systems working together and synergistically. Moreover, the focus in this section is on data, as there are different types of problems with data. On one hand, there is such a thing as too much data that does not lead to any significant business insights; on the other, many small and medium-sized companies complain of lack of access to qualitative data. There is also a difference between big and smart data and multiple small data sets that are not actionable. We will discuss the ways of addressing this barrage of data and reducing the noise, and present examples of failures stemming from spurious correlations. We will also mention some alternative approaches to data collecting and processing, such as data minimalism.

Section 10 tries to predict the unpredictable: the distant future of AI. In 2019, information about "xenobots" (Ramanujam et al. 2022) – artificial, but biological proto-organisms – was overwhelmed in the news cycle by the coronavirus pandemic. We know proteins are by far the best hardware for information processing. Is synthetic biology combined with AI capable of introducing a paradigm change? What will be the consequences? What is beyond deep learning? Is another AI revolution on the horizon?

We conclude with some final remarks and recommended readings provided by GPT-3. We will also explain how we trained and used AI in researching and writing this Element. It is our hope that this work contributes to a better and broader understanding of AI's place in business and organizational strategy, beyond purely competitive advantages and moving in the direction of collaboration and decentralized, networked approaches. This is our element.

2 AI Is Here. What Now?

TL;DR GPT summary: AI is definitely here to stay and is only going to become more and more prevalent in our lives. It is important to be realistic about its potential and its limitations. As with any new technology, there will be a period of adjustment as we learn how to use it effectively.

Remember the excitement when Deep Blue defeated Kasparov at chess? It was the first defeat of a reigning chess champion by a computer in a tournament, and possibly the beginning of AI fervor (Newborn 2012). What we often forget is that this chess match took place in 1997. Does it mean that AI technology has not advanced since then? Not really.

Since Deep Blue's defeat of Kasparov, there have been many breakthroughs in the field of AI. While a computer defeating a human chess master was a huge accomplishment, it was only the beginning.

Since then, AI has advanced by leaps and bounds. It has been used in a variety of fields, from medical diagnosis to translations to facial recognition. While humans are still better at computers when it comes to creative tasks, there are many tasks that AI can now do at least as well as humans. As Amara's Law states, "we tend to overestimate the effect of a technology in the short run and underestimate the effect in the long run" (Brooks 2017). This is definitely the case with AI. In the short run, we might see AI as a fad. However, in the long run, AI is only going to become more prevalent. It is also worth noting that the first predictions, that machines would be beating humans at chess within a decade, were made in the late 1950s (Simon and Newell 1958). While it took computers much longer than that, recent successes with much more complicated games, such as Go, show that the pace of growth for AI has been impressive.

The Go game has been a challenge for AI developers. The game has numerous possible move sequences and can be difficult for machines to master. The game is also played on a board with 19 lines and 19 rows, meaning that there are 361 possible moves. In recent years, machine learning has been used to develop programs that can play Go. These programs have learned how to play Go by analyzing the moves of professional players. In 2016, Google's AlphaGo program defeated a world champion Go player, Lee Sedol, in a five-game match. The match was a significant victory for AI, and Lee Sedol has retired from professional play, declaring AI invincible. In 2017, Google's AlphaGo program defeated world champion Ke Jie in a three-game match (Bory 2019).

In 2018, AlphaGo Zero – a program developed by Google DeepMind – defeated a world champion Go player Ke Jie in a three-game match. What makes AlphaGo Zero's victory so remarkable is that it learned the game from scratch, by playing against itself. This milestone shows that machine learning can now solve problems that humans may not have considered. In other words, AlphaGo Zero had nothing to learn from humans, which is a sobering thought. This was possible thanks to deep learning, a form of machine learning that is based on artificial neural networks. It differs from regular machine learning and AI in its ability to learn from unstructured or unlabeled data. This allows it to learn at a much deeper level than other machine-learning algorithms. Deep learning is a powerful tool for solving complex problems, and has been used to create self-driving cars, improve medical diagnoses, and much more. In gaming, AI technology has recently taken two major steps, by beating humans in poker (Romer 2022), a game traditionally perceived as requiring intuition and the ability to "read" other players, and bridge (Spinney 2022), a team game that many considered to be one of the last bastions of human superiority over machines (Mahalingam 2017). In Table 1, we summarize the differences between different types of machine learning: unsupervised learning, supervised learning, and reinforcement learning.

There is no escaping the point that every company will have to rely on AI technology soon or go out of business. In the late 1990s, Oracle's business website, oracle.com/ebusiness, announced "Five years from now, no one will call it e-business; it will simply be business." In 2000, PriceWaterhouseCooper ran an ad stating "The name for E-Business in the year 2000 will simply be: Business." While these predictions were a couple of years off, the direction was spot-on: No industries or businesses can thrive without a digital component, so there is simply no business without e-business. The same can be said of AI.

"AI in Business" will soon simply be "Business." To be successful in AI, you need to think about how AI can help you take advantage of new business opportunities. Let's say your company offers e-commerce services, but you can't compete against Amazon. You might need to rethink your business model, perhaps becoming the platform for other e-commerce sellers (eBay). Maybe you can be the platform for e-commerce sellers and for logistics companies to coordinate with each other (Alibaba). Without implementing some AI solutions, you will not be able to keep up, just as traditional businesses that ignored the IT

Table 1 Different types of machine learning

	Machine learning	
Unsupervised learning	**Supervised learning**	**Reinforcement learning**
A type of machine learning where the data is not labeled, and the algorithm is left to discover patterns in the data. Some common unsupervised learning algorithms are:	A type of machine learning whereby the model is trained using labeled data. Supervised learning is generally more accurate than unsupervised learning, as the model is able to learn from the specific information provided in the labels. However, it is also more time *consuming*, as labeling data can be a lengthy process.	A type of machine learning that enables an agent to learn in an interactive environment by trial and error using feedback from its own actions and the environment. It is more accurate than supervised learning and can adapt to changing situations more quickly, but requires even more resources.
- Clustering algorithms (e.g., k-means)	Some common examples of supervised learning algorithms are:	Some common examples of reinforcement learning algorithms are:
- Association rule learning (e.g., Apriori)	- Linear regression	- Q-learning
- Dimensionality reduction (e.g., principal component analysis)	- Logistic regression	- SARSA
	- Support vector machines	- TD learning
	- Decision trees	- Monte Carlo methods
	- Random forests	
Business applications include:		Business applications include:
- Big Data visualizations	Business applications include:	- Real-time decisions,
- Feature elicitation	- Image classification	- AI games
- Targeted marketing and recommendation systems	- Fraud detection	- Customer service chatbots
- Customer segmentation	- Customer retention	- Predicting financial markets

revolution closed their doors. In a 2021 survey of Fortune 1000 C-suite executives, 77.8 percent of the companies that responded reported either already using or introducing AI solutions in their core business (Bean 2021).

Porter (2001) wrote that "[M]any have argued that the Internet renders strategy obsolete. In reality, the opposite is true. Because the Internet tends to weaken industry profitability without providing proprietary operational advantages, it is more important than ever for companies to distinguish themselves through strategy." The same can be said of AI in strategy.

One successful example of using AI in strategy is Uber. Uber has used AI to transform not only its own business, but also to improve its customer service, make it easier for customers to find and book rides, and offer customers discounts and promotions. Uber has also used AI to improve its own operations, by making it easier for drivers to find and pick up fares, and by using AI to dispatch drivers to areas where demand is highest.

Naturally, AI technology cannot solve all of our problems or magically make us all more productive. We need to be realistic about its potential and its limitations. As with any new technology, there will be a period of adjustment as we learn how best to use it.

One challenge with AI is that it can be difficult to explain how it works. This "black box" problem is compounded by the fact that many AI applications are built on top of existing systems, making it hard to understand how AI interacts with them. For example, a chatbot might use AI to decide how to respond to a customer inquiry, but it is using rules written by humans. If the chatbot gives a response that does not answer the customer's question, it can be hard to figure out whether the problem is with the AI or with the rules. Another challenge is that AI is often used to automate decision-making, but it can be difficult to determine when and how to use AI rather than a person to make a decision. Sometimes AI is preferable because it has access to more data or can process that data faster, but at other times, a person is better. As Andrew Ng, a pioneer of AI, once put it, "If a typical person can do a mental task with less than one second of thought, we can probably automate it using AI either now or in the near future" (Strickland 2016).

The term AI was coined by John McCarthy (1955), who defined it as "the science and engineering of making intelligent machines." AI is a field of computer science that is concerned with the design and development of intelligent computer systems. AI research explores ways to answer the question of how to create computers that are capable of intelligent behavior. AI is related to the field of machine learning, which studies the question of how to create computer programs that automatically improve with experience: algorithms that can learn from and make predictions on data. There is no single definition of AI, and the field is constantly evolving. However, there are some common themes and goals that researchers in AI strive for, such as developing machines that can reason, learn, and solve problems like humans do. Consequently, AI can be used to implement problem-solving and knowledge-based systems, expert systems, NLP, and robotics. So when we talk about AI, we are referring to a broad category of distinct technologies. In Table 2, we summarize the ten key areas in which AI is developing: neural networks, genetic algorithms, fuzzy logic, probabilistic reasoning, decision trees, support vector machines, Bayesian networks, expert systems, natural language processing, and robotics. While AI may make significant advances in one of these areas, it may be developing at a more modest pace in others. Treating AI as a catch-all term is often misleading.

Another common typology of AI systems refers to their advancement level and includes reactive machines, limited memory, theory of mind, and self-awareness. Reactive machines are the simplest form of AI, and they can only react to their environment. Limited memory machines are more elaborate, and can remember and use experiences to make decisions. Theory of mind machines are even more complex, and can understand and predict the behavior of other entities. Self-awareness machines are the most sophisticated form of AI, and are aware of their own existence and can act accordingly.

Whether we will ever create fully self-aware machines is a matter of intensive debate. Ilya Sutskever, an OpenAI researcher, tweeted that "it may be that today's large neural networks are slightly conscious" (Sutskever 2022). Others believe that we will never reach this level of advancement (Kak 2019; Li, He, and Guo 2021), or that consciousness does not matter for AI, even though it may for philosophers (Hildt 2019).

Consciousness, however, may actually also be gradable. Three levels are commonly described. Level C0 is what researchers call "access consciousness." It's the level at which our brains register information from our environment. It doesn't require any awareness. For example, if you hear a loud noise, your brain will take in the sound, even if you're not paying attention. The second level of consciousness is "primary consciousness." At this level, we are aware of our surroundings and can focus on certain stimuli. This is the level at which we consciously perceive our world. The third and final level of consciousness is "higher-order consciousness." This is the level at which we are aware of our thoughts and feelings and can reflect on our mental states. In short, we are self-aware. To create truly conscious AI, we need to design machines that are capable of all three levels of consciousness. The three-level framework provides a way of thinking about the problem that is both scientifically rigorous and accessible to nonspecialists.

Table 2 Ten fields of AI

Neural networks	Computer programs that mimic the workings of the human brain. They "learn" by example, and can be trained to recognize patterns of input (like images, sounds, and text) and to produce desired outputs (like predictions, classifications, and recommendations). Neural networks were first proposed in the 1940s, but only began to be widely used in AI in the 1980s. Today they are the technology at the heart of deep learning, and are used for tasks like image and voice recognition, machine translation, and autonomous vehicles.
Genetic algorithms	A type of optimization algorithm that is inspired by natural selection. They are commonly used to find solutions to problems that are too difficult to solve using traditional methods. Genetic algorithms work by starting with a population of potential solutions (called "chromosomes") and then applying a series of operators (such as mutation, crossover, and selection) to the population. These operators are designed to mimic the natural process of evolution, and over time the population of chromosomes "evolves" to become better and better at solving the problem.
Fuzzy logic	A type of logic that allows for degrees of truth. In classical Boolean logic, propositions are either true or false, with no middle ground. In fuzzy logic, propositions can be partially true or partially false. Fuzzy logic was first proposed in the 1960s and has been widely used in AI since the 1980s. It is particularly well-suited to applications like control systems, where a precise Boolean logic approach is not possible or desirable.
Probabilistic reasoning	A method of reasoning that takes into account the uncertainty of events. It is often used in AI applications where the data is incomplete or ambiguous and a precise Boolean logic approach is not possible or desirable. Probabilistic reasoning works by assigning probabilities to events and then using those probabilities to make predictions or decisions. For example, a medical expert might use probabilistic reasoning to diagnose a patient based on a set of symptoms.

Decision trees	A type of machine-learning algorithm that is used for both classification and regression tasks. They work by learning a set of rules that map input values (such as features of an image) to output values (such as the class label of the image). Decision trees are a popular method for machine learning, due to their interpretability, flexibility, and robustness. They are often used in applications like credit scoring and fraud detection.
Support vector machines	A type of machine-learning algorithm that is used for both classification and regression tasks. They work by learning a set of rules that map input values (such as features of an image) to output values (such as the class label of the image). Support vector machines are a popular method for machine learning, due to their interpretability, flexibility, and robustness. They are often used in applications like credit scoring and fraud detection.
Bayesian networks	A type of probabilistic graphical model that is used for both classification and regression tasks. They work by learning a set of rules that map input values (such as features of an image) to output values (such as the class label of the image). Bayesian networks are a popular method for machine learning, due to their interpretability, flexibility, and robustness. They are often used in applications like credit scoring and fraud detection.
Expert systems	A type of AI that is designed to solve problems that require human expertise. They typically consist of two parts: a knowledge base, which contains information about the problem domain, and an inference engine, which uses the knowledge base to solve problems. Expert systems were one of the first AI applications to be developed, and were widely used in the 1980s and 1990s. They are still in use today, particularly in domains like medicine and finance.

Table 2 (cont.)

Natural language processing	Natural language processing (NLP) is a subfield of AI that deals with the processing of natural language data. Natural language data can include text, speech, and handwriting. NLP is a complex field, and involves tasks like text classification, text generation, and question answering. NLP is used in a variety of applications, such as machine translation, chatbots, and voice recognition.
Robotics	A subfield of AI that deals with the design and control of robots. Robots are often used to automate tasks that are difficult or dangerous for humans to perform. Robotics is a complex field, and involves tasks like motion planning, path planning, and object manipulation. Robotics is used in a variety of applications, such as manufacturing, healthcare, and disaster response.

For all practical purposes, there are a few problems with measuring self-aware AI. The first problem is that it's hard to define self-awareness. Some people think that self-awareness is just being aware of one's own thoughts and feelings. Others think it's being aware of one's existence. The second problem is that self-awareness is hard to measure. The tests to measure self-awareness are flawed. For example, the "mirror test" involves showing an AI a mirror and seeing if it recognizes itself. This test doesn't work with all forms of AI. Some AI can pass the test, but they're not actually self-aware, they're just good at recognizing patterns. The third problem is that it's hard to tell if self-awareness is real or not, because AI can fake self-awareness. The best-known AI tests are the Turing test, the Winograd schema challenge (WSC), and the Chinese room experiment.

The Turing test, designed by Alan Turing (1950), assesses a machine's ability to exhibit intelligent behavior equivalent to, or indistinguishable from, that of a human. It is widely used in AI research. The test works by having a human judge interact with two entities, one of which is a machine. If the judge cannot tell which is which, then the machine is said to have passed the test. The test is not perfect, because a machine can trick the judge without actually being intelligent. It is also possible for a human to fool the judge. Since the test is not very precise, there is no clear consensus whether chatbots are already at this level, but as early as 1972 some programs were able to fool some humans (Johnson 2022).

The Winograd schema challenge (WSC) was developed by Hector Levesque, a computer scientist from the University of Toronto (Levesque 2014), and named after Terry Winograd, a professor of computer science at Stanford University, who first proposed the use of such questions in testing AI. Designed to be an improvement on the Turing test, it is a multiple-choice test that uses specific questions known as Winograd schemas. A program has to answer questions about short stories, based on a set of given facts. To answer the questions correctly, the program must be able to understand the story. The WSC has been praised for its potential to evaluate a machine's true understanding of language, as opposed to its ability to recognize patterns or keywords. The test has been used in studies evaluating the performance of several AI systems, including Google's Parsey McParseface, IBM Watson, and Microsoft's Cortana. A sample WSC question is: "The man couldn't lift his son because he was so heavy. Who was heavy?" Most AI systems cannot answer this kind of WSC question, even though most humans have no difficulty doing so.

The Chinese room is a thought experiment proposed by philosopher John Searle (1980). It is intended to show that computers cannot think, at least not as humans do. The experiment is based on the following scenario: A person is locked in a room with a computer. There are no windows and no communication with the outside world. The person is given a set of rules about what to do for any given character in Chinese, a language that the person does not understand. The person is then given a piece of paper with a Chinese character on it. The person looks up the rule for that character and follows it. The result is another Chinese character, which the person passes on. The person in the room does not understand Chinese, but can follow the rules and produce the desired result, and appear to be able to communicate in Chinese, passing the Turing test if the provided rules are good enough.

Searle argues that this experiment shows that computers cannot think, and can follow rules without understanding them. Still, it is worth mentioning that current developments in the field are likely going far beyond what Searle imagined in the 1980s. Bidirectional Encoder Representations from Transformers (BERT) is a neural network from Google that is trained on large amounts of data to learn how to communicate in natural language. The project has shown that computers can be trained to understand text on a level that was previously possible only for humans. This is a significant advancement in the field of Natural Language Processing. An even more advanced model has been released in 2022: Pathways Language Model (PaLM) from Google is a text-processing and text-generating 540-billion-parameter transformer-based system, which, according to its creators, beats other state-of-the-art solutions, such as OpenAI's GPT-3, Nvidia and Microsoft's Megatron-Turing NLG, and DeepMind's Chinchilla and Gopher language models in many tasks, including question-and-answer, reading comprehension or commonsense reasoning. We should expect new and more advanced models to be released over the next decade, getting closer to effective machine communication. And even if a computer, like many people, can never fully grasp the semantics of something, it is possible that it would only provide a minimal difference for all practical purposes.

So, how do we know if an AI is really self-aware? We don't. We can only make educated guesses. Things are even worse when we remember that AI is a field rife with snake-oil sales, and marketing smoke and mirrors.

3 AI Evangelism and Snake Oil Sales

TL;DR GPT summary: AI is often misunderstood and overhyped. AI is still in its early stages of commercialization. It is important to understand precisely what we are going to use AI for. Focusing on low-hanging fruit instead of shooting for the moon is key. AI will have a transformative impact on all industries.

One problem with AI is that everyone understands it differently. As we noted in the previous section, the term itself is used in many ways, and its meaning has evolved over time. Some algorithms that are currently considered to be statistical data analytics (such as linear or nonlinear regression or multivariate regression) were perceived as the domain of AI decades ago. Even now, many companies combine traditional mathematical approaches with data and sell them as based on machine language (ML). Such approaches are not necessarily bad, but they are neither AI nor ML. They are just traditional mathematical models that are enhanced with data.

A 2019 survey conducted by MMC, a venture capital company, showed that approximately 40 percent of startups in Europe positioning themselves as AI startups do not actually use AI, at least not in any way material to their value proposition (Ventures 2019). This is likely because everything sounds better with "AI" in it. AI has become "the decade's worst buzzword" (Williams 2017). The market for AI is also growing fast, and it exceeded US$62 billion in 2021 (Grand View Research 2021), even though after a decade of "AI washing" some investors are a little more skeptical about it (Sanchez 2020; Schmelzer 2020). In many respects, AI is the snake oil of our time.

AI is hyped for several reasons. Sometimes people use the term "AI" when they really have something else in mind. For example, a company might describe a simple chatbot or a basic predictive analytics tool as "AI." Sometimes companies overpromise on what their AI technology can do. They make exaggerated claims about the technology's capabilities, or suggest that it can do things that it really can't. Sometimes we can observe "pseudo AI," or "The Wizard of Oz technique," with humans masquerading as fully autonomous AI systems. An early example of this was the "Mechanical Turk" chess-playing machine, invented in the eighteenth century. The machine was actually operated by a hidden human chess player. The hoax fooled people for many years. A more recent controversy involves Google's AI voice assistant: The voice assistant, "Google Home" was revealed to be human-powered. The voice assistant would answer users' questions, but some of the answers were provided by humans, not by AI. This revelation caused some backlash, as users thought that the company had misled them into believing that the voice assistant was powered exclusively by AI.

However, the situation is not so simple: Training an AI-powered voice assistant algorithm does require human feedback, review, and continuous supervised input. In fact, this is a legitimate way of "supercharging" AI (Metz 2015). Another controversy was caused by the demonstration of Google Duplex, which, in principle, was supposed to make AI-driven reservation calls on behalf of the phone owner. The presentation was impressive, but the AI dialogues may have been partially staged (Primack 2018).

Finally, some functions or products may be marketed as AI-based, although they rely only on some simple AI-related tools. For example, a company might sell an AI image recognition system or a spaced-repetition teaching program as ML-based. The problem is that these products might use some AI techniques, but they are not AI products. Similarly, a company that uses neural networks is not automatically an AI company (Frank 2017). It is worth noting though that this is a common marketing tactic, and it's not limited to AI. It's a way of making a product sound more impressive than it is.

In practice, the sophistication of existing technologies may be a matter of dispute and intensive marketing. For instance, in 2016, Elon Musk declared that all Tesla vehicles had all the hardware necessary for Level 5 autonomy, meaning full driving automation (SAE 2021). There were even videos, seemingly posted by Tesla enthusiasts, showing the excellent performance of the Autopilot system. Later it was discovered that these spontaneous videos may have been shot by Tesla employees, and the routes may have been mapped ahead of time in 3D (Metz and Boudette 2021). The company itself admitted overstating the car's abilities to the California Department of Motor Vehicles (PlainSite 2021). Sadly, the marketing of Teslas as almost ready for Level 5 autonomy appears to have been deceptive, but consistent with the company's habit of overstating the capabilities of its AI technology (Niedermeyer 2019), despite where AI technology currently is (Dickson 2020). In fact, at the time of writing this Element in 2022, there are no indications whatsoever that any vehicle currently produced is even remotely close to Level 5; the technology of autonomous vehicles is still in its infancy.

Elon Musk, however, is branding himself as an AI and tech visionary, developing other ventures with brave claims. His Neuralink, a brain implant that he touts as solving "paralysis, blindness, hearing," in the future, is called "neuroscience theater" by experts (Regalado 2020), and treated with the highest suspicion in terms of actual breakthrough results potential (Kirsch 2022), although possibly useful in niche applications (Behm 2022). Admittedly, Musk's unconventional style may have advantages outside marketing: While the hyped breakthroughs do not happen on schedule, they may happen sooner, as a result of the radical vision.

The best way to avoid AI snake oil is to be careful about the companies you do business with and to do your own research. Find out as much as you can about any company that you are thinking of working with, and familiarize yourself with its technology. And if you're thinking about using AI technology yourself, make sure you understand what it is and what it can (and cannot) do. Above all, don't fall for the hype.

Some advances in AI advances are truly breathtaking. To give just one recent example, AI-synthesized faces are not only indistinguishable from real ones but also more trustworthy (Nightingale and Farid 2022), which unsurprisingly results in a barrage of fake marketing-bot profiles on websites such as LinkedIn (Vigliarolo 2022). This is so because we are still figuring out what is and isn't possible – and ethical – with AI. We're also still figuring out what is and isn't economically viable. The last challenge is that AI is still very much in the early stages of commercialization. There are many startups and plenty of venture capital flowing into AI, but not many companies have figured out how to make money from AI.

This is why it is essential to understand precisely how we are going to use AI. For cost-cutting? Improving margins? Increasing revenues? Automated customer service can help reduce support costs while improving customer satisfaction. Predictive maintenance can help reduce downtime and improve equipment utilization. Intelligent pricing can help optimize pricing strategies and improve margins. Automated marketing can help improve customer acquisition and retention rates. Automated chatbots can handle simple customer queries, freeing up human customer service representatives to resolve more complex issues. Automated fraud detection can protect the bottom line. All of these are legitimate goals, but business strategy is the art of making painful choices among viable options. Deciding which approach reaps the most benefits is difficult.

Moreover, neat theoretically possible concepts and strong hunches do not translate into products. Many good ideas never get out of the concept phase simply because of tiny budgets. A lot of AI seed funding allows creating a prototype, but recruiting a highly skilled team to run the project long-term is a different game. And you need different specialists, too, because there are distinct professions in the field. You need a data engineer to get the data in the right format. Then, you need a data scientist to build the model. A data scientist is fantastic at statistics and modeling, but not necessarily good at writing code, so you also need a software engineer to write the code to put it into production. When you are developing your AI muscle, attend to the things that are achievable within your time and budget constraints first, and leave the bells and whistles for later.

As Thomas H. Davenport and Rajeev Ronanki (2018) point out, focusing on low-hanging fruit instead of aiming at moon shots is key: at least over the next couple of years even small AI projects can reap a lot of benefits, while bearing a much lower risk of utter failure.

Make no mistake here, though. The ball is already rolling. According to Gartner, AI will create $2.9 trillion of business value and 6.2 billion hours of worker productivity globally in 2022. According to McKinsey, AI will contribute up to $13 trillion to the global economy by 2030. According to PwC, AI could add $15.7 trillion to the global economy by 2030. According to Accenture, AI could increase annual economic growth rates in twelve developed economies by 0.8 percentage points, or $8.3 trillion, by 2035. According to Deloitte, AI will contribute $2 trillion to the Indian economy by 2030. According to Capgemini, AI will contribute $1.2 trillion to the global economy by 2025. The big picture is clear: AI is going to have a transformative impact on all industries.

This might explain why Google, currently competing with Microsoft shifting to becoming an "AI-First" company. The AI-First approach is a new way of thinking about how to use AI to create value. It is a shift from using AI to automate existing processes or improve existing products to using AI to create new ones; from using AI to make existing businesses more efficient to using AI to create new businesses. The AI-First approach is about using AI to create value that does not exist today, for customers, employees, and shareholders. It is important to keep some key points in mind (Amsalem 2022):

1. Make AI the center of the business, relying on strong executive support, and breaking with the traditional divisions. Organizations should focus on creating an AI-centric culture that is open to new ideas, willing to experiment, and focused on continuous learning. This can be done by establishing an AI Center of Excellence (CoE) that is responsible for identifying and championing AI initiatives, sharing best practices, and providing training and guidance to teams across the organization.
2. Make AI work in the long run, rather than focusing on perfect conditions for a one-time prediction or model. It is difficult to transition from research to production, and even more difficult to manage a consistent stream of reliable data. Google Flu's rise to fame and then failure is just one of many examples of how it works.[1]
3. Focus on the business problem, not the technology. It is essential to focus on the business problem that AI is meant to solve. Data scientists often get caught up in the technology and the possibilities of what can be done, rather than what should be done. The goal is to solve a business problem, not to create the coolest AI application.

---

[1] Google Flu failed because it was not able to accurately predict the spread of the flu. The project was based on the assumption that people who search for certain terms on Google are more likely to be sick, but this turned out not to be the case. Google Flu appeared to be a huge success initially though: Google Flu Trends (GFT) correctly predicted flu activity in the first year well within 10 percent of the CDC's weekly estimates in the United States. However, the accuracy of the predictions decreased over time, and, by 2012, the predictions were off by up to 50 percent. Google stopped publishing flu predictions in August 2015. There are several potential reasons why the Google Flu project failed. One possibility is that people's search behavior changed over time, and they were no longer using Google to look up information about the flu. Another possibility is that the algorithm used to predict flu activity was not accurate. Finally, it is also possible that the data collected by Google was not representative of the population as a whole. It is worth noting that Google Flu Trends paved the way for public health surveillance systems, and that, for example, food poisoning detection can be done much better than through traditional methods when using ML (Sadilek et al. 2018).

4. Automate data preparation. Data preprocessing and cleaning can be tedious and does not scale well. Put emphasis on automating data pipelines.
5. Use ready-made off-the-shelf AI solutions that are well tested and supported, but also keep improving. There is a plethora of open-source solutions, ready to be applied. Develop only the systems that cannot be easily acquired from the market.
6. Don't forget the humans. AI is not meant to replace humans, but to complement them. Keep the human element in mind when designing AI applications. For example, when designing a chatbot, consider how the chatbot will interact with humans. Will it be able to understand human emotions? How will it handle unexpected inputs? How will it know when to escalate to a human? These are all important considerations.
7. Manage expectations when it comes to AI. Many people have unrealistic expectations of what AI can do and how quickly it can do it. Set and manage realistic expectations throughout the project.
8. Keep optimizing the infrastructure decisions. With endless combinations of hardware, SaS (Software as Service), cloud solutions, et cetera, the overhead of load balancing and integrating them becomes one of the key costs of AI implementation.

4 Techno-realism: Red Pill, Blue Pill – You Don't Have to Choose

TL;DR GPT summary: AI is a powerful technology that has the potential to drastically change our lives for better or for worse. While there are many potential risks associated with AI, such as job losses, privacy issues, disinformation, and weaponization, there are also many potential benefits. It is important to remember that AI is still in its early stages and that many of the risks associated with it are not yet fully realized. We need to be careful with how we use AI and make sure that we are aware of the potential risks.

"AI is a fundamental risk to the existence of human civilization," Elon Musk said at the National Governors Association Summer Meeting in 2017 (Domonoske 2017). He called it a bigger threat than North Korea (David 2017). In the same spirit, according to the world-renown scientist, Stephen Hawking, "the development of full artificial intelligence could spell the end of the human race" (Luckerson 2014). No other than Bill Gates himself expressed major concerns about this technology (Kohli 2015). James Barrat (2013) wrote a book with the ominous title *Our Final Invention: Artificial Intelligence and the End of the Human Era*, in which he showed that many other notable technology experts also perceive AI as an existential threat.

We do not want to dispute any of these warnings. Yet, we want to offer a glimmer of hope: Terminator-like scenarios do not necessarily have to play out just yet. There is no doubt that AI will have a huge impact on many aspects of our lives, and surely it is important to consider the potential risks and benefits of this technology as it develops. We want to discuss the common fears associated with AI, and the common hopes, and ultimately offer a balanced view on the topic.

Some potential risks of AI include job losses, privacy issues, disinformation, overdependence on technology, weaponization, and superintelligence. We address them here in more detail.

Job Losses: As AI and automation become more advanced, there is a risk that many jobs will be replaced by machines. This could lead to mass unemployment and a decrease in the standard of living for many people. In fact, AI is, beyond doubt, a highly disruptive technology, and we need to realize that it likely will lead to many jobs being entirely redundant – be it in customer service and telemarketing, manufacturing, logistics, finance, paralegal jobs, or media (Girasa 2020). However, AI development will also lead to **job creation**: As AI and automation become more advanced, there is a potential for new types of jobs to be created. This could lead to increased employment and a higher standard of living for many people. Fear mongering about AI taking all of our jobs in the near-term future is more of a domain of populist politics than reality (Levy 2018). And in the long run, there are simply too many factors to account for, but the fact that automation may lead to all of us having to work less does not necessarily have to be a bad thing. The problem may not be with the reduction of the number of jobs, but with the economic consequences – and there are many ongoing discussions on how to address the problem of mass unemployment, with Universal Basic Income considered to be one of the promising solutions (Wright and Przegaliñska 2021 promising, yet controversial solutions).

Privacy Issues: As AI is used to gather and process data, there is a risk that personal information could be mishandled or leaked. This could have a negative impact on people's privacy and security. It is true that the mind-blowing intrusions to our privacy available thanks to new technologies, including AI, are a serious risk even to democracy itself (Manheim and Kaplan 2019), and the Cambridge Analytica scandal has likely been just the tip of an iceberg. While it is convenient to board a plane without the need to show ID, the situation in which most of the time all of our moves are tracked, videotaped, and cross-analyzed with our purchases and even bodily movements is scary. Still, while technological possibilities are developing fast and regulation naturally lags behind, it is still largely a regulatory issue, and ethical and legal discussions about what should be allowed and what not are ongoing (Zhang, Mengjia et al. 2021). The interplay between personalization and privacy is not in equilibrium, but there already are solutions for human- and privacy-centric approaches to AI (Beduschi 2021). Ultimately, assuming that privacy is dead is likely not productive, as we as a society decide through our laws what is permissible and acceptable, including the scope of surveillance and privacy erosion. Also, while there are many ethical challenges to solve, it is also clear that mass personalization, resulting from AI use, has a lot of social good potential as well (Hermann 2021; Banker and Khetani 2019).

Disinformation: There is a risk that AI could be used to create "fake news" or to spread disinformation. As AI technology scales much better than human teams cost-wise, and as it can be highly adaptive and viral, and perpetuate and promote only the kinds of misinformation that have the highest impact, the risk is definitely real. This could have a negative impact on society and on people's ability to make informed decisions. We can see this happening already: deepfakes of politicians are spread to sow doubt, AI-driven networks of bots perpetuate misinformation, and even traditional media on occasion get involved (Jemielniak and Krempovych 2021). However, we need to remember that disinformation has been a part of political repertoire since the beginnings of our civilization: for instance, Octavius successfully used it against Marcus Antonius (Kouroutakis 2019). Arguably, the current problem with advancing network propaganda (Benkler, Faris, and Roberts 2018) has at least as much to do with the social media and platforms as with the AI technology itself. Moreover, there are several ways to mitigate this risk. We can educate people on how to spot fake news, we can develop algorithms that can detect fake news (Ozbay and Alatas 2020), and we can create policies that discourage the spread of fake news and their monetization by social networks.

Dependence on Technology: As we become increasingly reliant on AI, there is a risk that we could become too dependent on technology. This could lead to problems if the technology fails or is not available. However, quite clearly, this is the case with any useful technology. In fact, most of us would not survive long without the industrial revolution inventions, or even the simplest IT systems that sustain our logistics, and the disruptions in distribution channels visible during the SARS-COV2 pandemic, as well as those resulting from sanctions on Russia are just two recent examples of this phenomenon. As we are arguing in this Element, AI is already permeating all industries and becoming a backbone of any business – but the same was true of the Internet, too. Thus, the main risks related specifically to AI could be some form of overdependence, yet these risks are no different than the risks associated with any other technology. And, true, we could also become too reliant on AI to make decisions for us. However, this is not necessarily a bad thing. It may mean that we get better outcomes, as AI can take into account more information than we can.

Algorithmic biases: Black box decision-making systems, such as AI-driven systems, by definition, are not transparent, even if they produce better results according to the specified criteria. This risk is definitely real and already happening: for instance, an AI algorithm denied 80 percent of black mortgage applications (Martinez 2021). The bias was not caused by the lack of capability of the AI system, but because of the lack of data to train the AI system. The system was not racist by design, it was just not trained with a diverse enough data set. There already are initiatives combating AI bias in such a situation, such as the MIT-based Black Loans Matter initiative, but it is definitely true that there is also a risk that a biased dataset will result in a biased AI system. This was definitely true of, for example, Microsoft Twitter chatbot, Tay, which learned the language from people on Twitter, and quickly skewed toward racist remarks (Schwartz 2019). Other forms of bias can be visible in HR software systems (Bogen 2019). For example, if an AI system is trained on a dataset of job applicants, and the dataset is biased against women, then the AI system will also be biased against women. An MIT researcher and the Founder of Algorithmic Justice League, Joy Buolamwini (2017) has shown that facial recognition systems are more accurate for white men than for darker-skinned women: Netflix has a great documentary, "Coded Bias," about the problem. We should also keep in mind that the results of AI–decision-making may also be biased because of the bias present in society and not the fault of technology, but rather the boundary conditions we impose on it. There are many ways to mitigate these risks. For example, organizations can use multiple data sets when training their AI systems, including data sets that are diverse in terms of race, gender, and other characteristics. Organizations can also audit their AI systems on a regular basis to ensure that they are performing as intended and that they are not biased. Also, these systems should not be used for high-stakes decisions: if anyone tries to persuade you that the atom bomb button should be in AI hands, tell them to back off the Kool-Aid. There are a few ways to mitigate these risks. One is to build in transparency and accountability from the start. For example, when training an AI system, we can keep track of which data points the system is using to make its decisions. This way, if the system is biased, we can identify which data points are causing the bias and adjust accordingly. Another way to mitigate the risk is to use a "human in the loop" approach, where a human is always involved in the final decision. For example, when a facial recognition system identifies a person as being of a certain race, the human can confirm or override that decision. Ultimately, though, the best way to mitigate the risk is to use AI systems for decision-making only when they are absolutely necessary. If a decision can be made without an AI system, then we should avoid using one.

Weaponization: There is a risk that AI could be used to create powerful weapons to harm people or even entire nations. This could lead to a new arms race and an increased risk of conflict. The US Department of Defense refers to weaponized AI as "Algorithmic warfare." "Maven" project, started by the Pentagon in 2017, is an early example of such warfare. The aim of Maven is to speed up the process of identifying targets from video footage and images by using machine-learning algorithms. Google was initially contracted to work on the project, but later pulled out due to ethical concerns. Other commercial companies, such as Amazon, IBM, or Microsoft, have offered their solutions to the military, and Russia is investing into Combat Robots, which are meant to serve autonomously instead of soldiers (Sisson et al. 2020). The British dystopian series, *Black Mirror*, addressed the threat of weaponized AI in a couple of episodes, showing, for example, that autonomous drones can be used by terrorists to attack civilians, or that autonomous military robots can go rogue and eliminate human civilization. While these risks are definitely real, it is important to note that so far AI has not been weaponized to a large extent, and that, just like with algorithmic bias, the scope of danger is entirely dependent on the controlling mechanisms we introduce. Without dismissing the threat of weaponized AI, we would also like to note that humanity already does possess weapons with a potential to annihilate our civilization, and we work around them, creating procedures for mitigating the risk (Pinker 2018).

Superintelligence: Some experts believe that AI could eventually surpass human intelligence, leading to a situation where machines are in control. This could have disastrous consequences for humanity. According to some authors, misaligned AI is one of four existential risks we ignore, the three others being solar flares,[2] supervolcanoes, and pandemics (Noy and Uher 2022). In theory, a possible way to control AI is to ensure that it is beneficial to humanity. This can be done in a number of ways, such as specifying that its goals should be aligned with human values, or building in a "kill switch" that can be used to shut it down if it becomes uncontrollable. However, even these measures may not be enough to control super-intelligent AI, and it is possible that the only way to ensure our safety

---

[2] If you are interested in the topic of solar flares threat, read more in the Wikipedia article on the Carrington Event: https://en.wikipedia.org/wiki/Carrington_Event, and on solar flare: https://en.wikipedia.org/wiki/Solar_flare.

is to avoid creating it in the first place. While all previous risks mentioned in this section can at least potentially be controlled, super-intelligent AI, by the very definition, cannot. All safeguards we can deploy will be no more effective than the safeguards our dogs may want to create to make sure we do not leave them at home: with the IQ differential that is too high, we can only hope AI will consider us to be cute enough to be saved. Novels such as *A Fire upon the Deep* by Vernon Vinge or *The Freeze-Frame Revolution* by Peter Watts show perfectly well that the problem with super-intelligent AI is that once it is created, it cannot be stopped; still, all steps leading to its creation are incremental, bring huge benefits, and may appear to be safe. As Oxford cryptologist I.J. Good observed as early as in 1966:

> Let an ultraintelligent machine be defined as a machine that can far surpass all the intellectual activities of any man however clever. Since the design of machines is one of these intellectual activities, an ultraintelligent machine could design even better machines; there would then unquestionably be an 'intelligence explosion,' and the intelligence of man would be left far behind. Thus, the first ultraintelligent machine is the last invention that man need ever make.

We are far from diminishing this risk. However, in this Element, we would like to offer a different perspective; as AI keeps evolving, humans adapt to new technologies. As Pedro Domingos (2015), observes in *The Master Algorithm*, humans may coevolve with AI, and keep augmenting themselves as technology advances. Even more interestingly, the development of AI may lead to us merging into new, posthuman species, blending with the AI. In any case, we definitely agree that assuming a "null hypothesis" – that the risks of superintelligence can keep being ignored – is problematic and that there is a strong need for analyzing the dangers and counter-strategies of the phenomenon (Bostrom 2015).

Overall, it is clear that AI is a powerful technology. Google CEO Sundar Pichai said that "AI is one of the most important things humanity is working on. It is more profound than, I dunno, electricity or fire" (Clifford 2018). Instead of utopian all-in praises or Luddite-like alarmist warnings, we need to focus on solutions, regulations, and control. Oversight over business-developed AI is especially needed, as it is currently lacking. With the rapid technological advancement of AI and the lack of understanding and regulation of it, we need to do something now to protect ourselves (Wischmeyer and Rademacher 2020).

5 Finding a Place for AI in Strategy

TL;DR GPT summary: AI can make a difference in strategy in terms of changes in understanding and optimizing internal processes and structures, the products and services the company offers, the distribution channels, and monetization of these products and services, market analysis, and understanding the customers.

AI products are everywhere, and in industries where they are least expected: An AI-driven robot from Miso Robotics, Flippy 2, can grill and flip perfect burgers. A RoboBEER AI-driven robot can pour a perfect beer, in terms of the bubble size, beer color, and temperature. Symrise, a German perfume producer, cooperates with IBM to use AI to analyze past blockbusters and devise new ones. Singapore-based Hoow Foods uses AI to develop new textures, tastes, and nutritional component proportions in sauces and ice cream. IntelligentX comes up with new beer flavors. For years, AI could even help write better rap lyrics (Malmi et al. 2015). Beauty.ai, backed by NVidia and EY, ran a global beauty pageant, with AI choosing the best-looking people, and now, pivoted to Haut.ai, automating the collection of high-resolution skin data. *Harry Potter and the Portrait of What Looked Like a Large Pile of Ash* was written by AI after the AI was fed the first four books of the Harry Potter series. It is clear that AI applications are entering unconventional fields. The question is no longer whether AI can be useful in some business applications. Rather, we need to focus on how to introduce it and, specifically, what AI approach will be most optimal for our strategy.

The impact of this transformation on business models will be profound. Even before AI, the improvements in efficiency brought by technology, as well the advancing specialization and the new knowledge-work professions have effectively resulted in horizontal specialization and much looser, networked structures (Jemielniak 2012). Vertical integration of the value chain is also becoming a rarity – it lacks flexibility, but even more importantly it does not allow building the competitive advantage mainly through focusing on the core competence (Mooney 2007). Today, companies like Apple do not produce any of their products. They outsource production to Foxconn, and even assembly is done in China. Apple only designs and markets the products. In the same way, Apple outsources the production of the iPhone screens to Samsung. Outsourcing everything that is non-core is a way of leveraging other companies' core competencies, and it is a fundamental principle of the new business model (Amit and Zott 2020). Due to the erosion of entry and exit barriers – with globalization of knowledge, it becomes easier than ever to enter the business (Oriesek and Schwarz 2020). Google, based on its core competencies and the network effect, was able to enter the business of mobile operating systems and gain a significant share of the market. At the same time, it is easy to exit the business. For example, Google killed its Reader service, because it was losing money. The company was able to recognize that it is not in its core competencies, and to exit from the business quickly (Schmidt and Rosenberg 2014). In fact, Google routinely evaluates its projects against the core mission and competence, and KilledByGoogle.com, a website dedicated to cataloging projects deprecated by Google, lists 267 so far.

We can see another side of such radical core competence focus on the rise of outsourcing and "platform" businesses such as Uber, which enable other firms to piggyback on their infrastructure and reach. This trend is likely to continue, as the costs of entry into many industries continue to fall and the benefits of scale and scope decrease.

In this landscape, it is particularly important to find a place for AI in strategy. Some could argue that it does not make any sense to adjust strategy to a technology. We addressed this point in previous sections, so we will just reiterate that companies without a clear vision of employing AI will be out of business, period. AI is not just another tech fad, it is a radical, transformative disruption. Perhaps it is too early to devise an AI strategy, as the changes are simply too dynamic. Yes, the changes are dynamic, but what does not change is the fact that companies have to have a clear vision of AI utilization. AI is not just a technology, it is a whole new way of operating. A company that does not have a clear vision of AI utilization will not survive. We no longer need a strategy *for* AI; we need a strategy *with* AI (Kiron and Schrage 2019).

The problem is that designing AI's place in strategy cannot be fully out-sourced. AI wizards can drive the technological part, but ultimately, the biggest challenge is leveraging AI to gain a competitive advantage specific to one's industry and strategic domain (Thompson and Cacal 2022). Getting to know more about AI in general, and AI in business, in particular, are crucial for a successful deployment of an AI strategy (Mauro and Valigi 2020).

The key areas in which AI can make a difference in the strategy include:

- understanding and optimizing internal processes and structures
- the products and services the company offers
- the distribution channels and monetization of these products and services
- market analysis and understanding the customers

Deloitte 2020's *State of AI in the Enterprise* describes the first two points as the most frequently mentioned top benefits that adopters of AI in business seek. At the same time, less than half of adopters believe they have a high level of skill in choosing the right AI technologies and suppliers, and about half think that their organization is slowing down AI strategy adoption because of the emerging risks. Additionally, it is worth considering that even though optimization of processes may be low-hanging fruit, it is going to be difficult to differentiate through it, as AI goes mainstream, and is also standardized in SaS (Software as Service).

In this light, we would like to argue a different point: that for organizations that have not invested in AI muscle noticeably yet, the lowest-hanging fruit may be actually employing it for business intelligence and market research, as well as optimizing the distribution channels and monetization of the products first.

Strategy, at its core, relies on managing uncertainty with the upcoming opportunities (Spender 2014). Artificial Intelligence systems that are built around pipelines of data acquired, scraped, or otherwise collected from the available sources are able to provide businesses with a timely, if not real-time, understanding of what is going on in their ecosystem (Bulusu and Abellera 2020). These systems are not restricted to understanding only the structured data, but also unstructured data, such as text, images, and video. Thus, they can be used to monitor social media, news, and other sources of information for sentiment analysis, as well as for identifying new trends. This information can be used to make better-informed decisions about where the company should direct its attention and resources. In other words, AI can be used to reduce uncertainty about the future and make the business more agile in the face of change. Moreover, starting with business intelligence (BI) and combining it with low-code or zero-code approaches makes a natural transition in AI scaling. We are going to cover these approaches later on, so let's just give one example here: Companies such as Akkio already offer decision-making engines based on a graphical interface with no code skills required, and this trend is going to boom in the coming years.

The following examples show how AI can be used to support strategic decision-making.

1. Market analysis: AI can be used to collect and analyze data about customer behavior, preferences, and needs. This information can be used to identify new market opportunities and to develop strategies for targeting these markets.

2. Customer segmentation: AI can be used to segment customers into groups based on their behavior, preferences, and needs. This information can be used to develop customized marketing and sales strategies for each segment.

3. Sales and marketing optimization: AI can be used to optimize sales and marketing campaigns by predicting which customers are most likely to respond positively to a given offer. This information can be used to target campaigns more effectively and to improve conversion rates.

4. Customer service optimization: AI can be used to improve customer service by predicting which customers are most likely to need help and by providing them with personalized assistance. This can be used to improve customer satisfaction and loyalty.

These steps can be taken with a small team and build on existing competence in business analytics. They also are data- rather than model-centric, which, even for now, offers better versatility of incremental system deployment. But there is more: Andrew Ng, a prominent AI expert, predicts that the coming decade is going to rely on a data-centric approach to AI (Anadiotis 2022). This means that data-driven methods, such as deep learning, will play a larger role in AI development than traditional rule-based systems. This shift will be driven by the increasing availability of data, which will allow data-driven methods to outperform traditional methods. To make this happen, businesses will need to develop more powerful AI systems that can learn from data more effectively, solve more complex problems, and provide better decision support. For now, we argue that steps 1–4 make for a reasonable entry approach to developing an AI strategy. More advanced steps should include understanding and optimizing internal processes and structures, and in particular:

5. Process optimization: AI can be used to optimize internal processes such as supply chain management, production planning, and inventory management. This can improve efficiency and reduce costs.
6. Organizational design: AI can be used to redesign organizational structures and processes to improve performance. This can be used to improve efficiency, productivity, and decision-making.
7. Change management: AI can be used to manage change within an organization, such as implementing new strategies, organizational structures, or processes. This can be used to ensure the successful and efficient implementation of changes.

These steps require more skill, and cannot rely solely on AI developers. In fact, pretty much like with traditional software development, they can prove successful if the top management knows exactly what is needed, what the boundary conditions are, what the technology allows, and what data can and should be used as inputs. Moreover, changes mentioned in steps 5–7 need to rely on a combined record of both quantitative data and qualitative inquiry, in a form of "Thick Big Data" (Jemielniak 2020).

Finally, the most advanced step will be altering the products and services the company offers, and ultimately developing new, AI-driven products and services. Examples of such endeavors could include:

8. Product and service development: AI can be used to develop new products and services that are tailored to customer needs and preferences by creating new designs, testing new products, or creating new marketing strategies. This can create a competitive advantage and to increase sales and revenue.
9. AI-driven products and services: AI can be used to develop products and services that are powered by AI. This can create a competitive advantage and to increase sales and revenue.

10. Platforms and ecosystems: AI can be used to develop platforms and ecosystems that are powered by AI. This can create a competitive advantage and increase sales and revenue.

These steps require much more significant investment and are likely to be successful only if the company has a clear understanding of its strengths and weaknesses, and of the opportunities and threats that it faces. Moreover, they require a significant investment of resources, both in terms of money and of skills and expertise.

In conclusion, AI can be a powerful tool for supporting strategic decision-making. However, it is important to understand that AI is not suitable for all organizations and situations. Moreover, AI is not a substitute for good strategic thinking, but rather a tool that can support it.

It is also worth remembering that, according to Boston Consulting Group, the companies that were able to leverage AI at scale, typically dedicate only 10 percent of their AI budget to algorithms, 20 percent to technologies, and as much as 70 percent to making sure that AI is well embedded into business processes. Perceiving AI as predominantly an investment in software or hardware is missing the point – the largest chunk of work that needs to be done lies in meaningful implementation.

On a final note, there is no one-size-fits-all approach to implementing AI in strategy, as the key to success with implementing AI in a business depends on the business and its specific needs. However, there are some general principles that can be useful for all businesses when it comes to implementing AI.

First, there must be a clear understanding of what AI can and cannot do. AI is a powerful tool, but it is not a panacea. It is important to understand the limitations of AI and not expect it to solve all the organization's problems. Second, it is important to have a clear understanding of the organization's goals and how AI can help to achieve them. AI should not be implemented for its own sake, but rather for the purpose of achieving specific business goals. Third, it is important to have the right team in place. This team should not only be composed of experts in AI, but also experts in the specific domain in which AI is being implemented. Fourth, it is important to have a clear plan for how AI will be implemented. This plan should take into account the specific needs of the organization and the specific goals that AI is meant to help achieve. Finally, it is important to monitor the results of AI implementation and to be prepared to make changes. AI is a dynamic field, and what works today may not work tomorrow.

Likewise, there are blind spots to look out for in AI strategy:

Dependence on a single data set. AI relies on data sets to learn from and improve. But if the data set is biased, or if it changes, the AI system will not be able to adapt. Machine-learning algorithms can succumb to bias if they are not fed an appropriate variety of data

Lack of transparency. AI systems are becoming increasingly sophisticated and opaque, meaning that it is difficult to understand how they arrived at their answers. This lack of transparency makes it hard to explain the decisions that they have arrived at and to improve them.

Analysis paralysis. As we argue in the previous section, there is such thing as too much data. AI, being a powerhouse for combining and crunching big datasets, can become an excuse for not thinking critically and independently, or even worse: for overthinking the problem without making a decision, when it is already due.

Misalignment with company culture and values. AI is not a value-neutral technology, and it is important to ensure that it is in line with the values of the organization. For example, if a company's values include transparency and accountability, then AI systems must be designed to be transparent and accountable.

Personal data privacy and security. AI systems depend on access to large amounts of personal data. This raises privacy and security concerns.

Lack of context. AI is so powerful that it is easy to forget that in can only operate in a narrow context – using an approach, which worked fine in one situation will not necessarily translate into working even remotely well in a similar situation. Humans are still much better at adaptation.

6 Competitive Advantage Reinvented

TL;DR GPT summary: This section focuses on the ways to compete in the digital age. Artificial intelligence, combined with other crucial technologies such as edge computing, may thoroughly transform business strategies as we know them. Companies that pioneer applying AI to their business processes are rapidly transforming not only their own operations, but the shape of the whole sector.

According to many distinguished experts, there are still two main ways to compete (Martin 2015): through "cost leadership" and "differentiation." This claim echoes Michael Porter's (1997) generic model. Additionally, as Porter later suggested, we can add "focus," understood as orientation on clearly defined groups of users and customers ("niches"), usually as an added layer to the two strategies mentioned.

Porter's strategic model has become an essential tool of strategic analysis and remained untouched, even though debated (Polo and Weber 2010; Magretta 2011)

throughout the previous waves of business transformations. Today, however, rapid technological pace allows us to review and potentially refine Porter's model.

As Porter argued, several decades ago, cost leadership was a strategy that involved being the low-cost producer in an industry. A firm following a cost leadership strategy seeks to attain the lowest cost position in its industry, given the range of product and service variations that it offers. The objective of cost leadership is to achieve economies of scale, that is, to reduce costs by increasing production. There are (or were) two ways to achieve cost leadership: either by producing on a large scale and achieving economies of scale (the more frequent option), or by using innovative technology that allows for lower production costs (the less frequent option).

Cost leadership can be a very effective strategy, but it has several disadvantages. It can be very difficult to achieve and maintain a cost advantage, because other companies will usually try to copy any cost-saving innovations. In addition, cost leadership can lead to a race to the bottom, where companies compete to undersell each other, which can damage the profitability of the entire industry.

Differentiation, in contrast, is a strategy that involves making a product or service unique in a way that is valued by customers. According to Porter's Generic Strategies (Porter 1997; Polo and Weber 2010), a company following differentiation offers products or services that are perceived as different from those of its competitors. Differentiation can be achieved in many ways, but some of the most common include offering unique products or services, providing superior customer service, or having a strong brand image (Islami et al. 2020). Porter emphasized that differentiation can be difficult to achieve and maintain. This is because other companies will try to copy any unique features that a company introduces. In addition, differentiation can lead to a high-cost strategy, as companies incur costs to make their products or services unique. Premium involves charging higher prices for a product or service than competitors. A company following a premium strategy seeks to be the high-price leader in its industry, offering products or services that are perceived as being of a higher quality than those of its competitors. Premium strategies can be very effective, but they have some important disadvantages. First of all, it can be very difficult to achieve and maintain a premium price advantage, again, because other companies will usually try to copy any unique features that a company introduces. In addition, premium strategies can lead to a high-cost strategy, as companies incur costs in order to make their products or services unique.

Interestingly, focus is understood as orientation on clearly defined groups of users/ customers (Porter and Gibbs 2001). This is a strategy that allows a company to be different and to meet the needs of a specific group of users.

In other words, focus means concentrating on and serving a narrow market segment and serving it better than anyone else. Focus approach is based on the assumption that it is easier to be the best in a narrow market segment than in the entire market. A focused company has chosen to limit its activities to a market niche. The main reason for this is that the company can better understand the needs of its target group and adapt its products and services to them. In addition, focused companies can more easily build a strong brand image associated with the target group.

Due to the accelerating pace of change in the technology landscape, Porter's model may be significantly transformed or, at least, made more granular. We should take into account that strategy is always a twofold effort: on one hand, it is focused on growing the company's core businesses and enhancing its product and service offerings to meet the needs of the customers; on the other hand, it is forward-looking and focused on expanding its customer base and growing its international business. Both directions are infused with emerging technologies in general, and AI in particular, and this process will become even more visible no matter the size of the organization and the sector it represents.

AI is having a significant impact on the business landscape. Being a broad field that includes areas such as machine learning, natural language processing, robotics, and more, certainly has the potential to transform healthcare, finance, manufacturing, and many other industries. In sectors like finance, the profundity of the change is already visible. Not only do machine-learning algorithms lead to optimization, but they change the strategic orientation of the key players who, more visibly than ever, want to build a strong predictive component into how they serve their customers and manage their processes. Businesses are using AI to automate tasks, improve decision-making, and develop new products and services (Acemoglu and Restrepo 2018). Several factors are now driving the growing use of AI in business. First, the cost of computing power and storage has fallen dramatically, making it more affordable for businesses to use AI. Second, the availability of data has increased exponentially, thanks to the growth of the Internet and the proliferation of sensors and devices. This data is a key input into AI algorithms. Finally, businesses are under pressure to compete in an increasingly global and dynamic marketplace, and they see AI as a way to gain a competitive advantage.

As there are many practical AI-based solutions in business, let us look at some examples. As mentioned before, AI can be used to develop more effective marketing campaigns by analyzing customer data to identify patterns and trends (Loureiro, Guerreiro, and Tussyadiah 2021). AI can also be used to develop new products or to customize existing products to meet the needs of specific customers.

AI can be used in human resources, to automate the recruitment and hiring employees, and to monitor employee performance and to identify training and development needs.

In supply chain management, AI can be used to optimize the flow of goods and materials through the supply chain, predict demand for products, and identify potential disruptions in the supply chain. It can also help to improve business operations by developing better algorithms for financial trading or to improve the accuracy of fraud detection ("Study: AI for Fraud Detection to Triple by 2021" n.d.;Soleymanzadeh et al. 2022).

How do these tailored solutions affect the direction of the whole organization? On a broader and more strategic level, AI can improve operational efficiency and reduce costs. For example, AI can automate tasks performed by human workers. This can free up human workers for other tasks or for redeployment to other areas of the business. AI can also improve the accuracy and speed of decision-making. For example, AI can be used to identify patterns and trends in data. This information can then inform decisions about where to allocate resources or what products to develop. AI can also help to create new products and services or improve existing ones. For example, AI can develop new marketing campaigns that are better targeted to customers, or develop new products or customize existing products to meet the needs of specific customers.[3]

This shows how two classic strategies can be redefined. Cost leadership can be transformed through automation of tasks, optimization of resources and increase in effectiveness. Differentiation starts to rely on personalized, or even hyper-personalized services and products through machine learning–enabled customer segmentation and targeted marketing. Moreover, focus may become the dominant strategy that organizes both cost leadership and differentiation approach. Machine learning, particularly unsupervised techniques like clustering (Domingos and Hulten 2001) or dimensionality reduction (Tenenbaum, de Silva, and Langford 2000), are all about focus. They allow for very refined analytics of people's purchasing decisions and shopping preferences to the degree where new products and services become hyper-personalized. Such products can lean toward premium, but they can also be very affordable. The costs of running unsupervised machine-learning models are dropping. Market actors can locate themselves both on the cost side and differentiation side.

---

[3] To support companies as they embark on their AI scale journeys, BCG (Strack et al. 2021) has developed an AI scale framework that guides organizations through the top ten areas of focus and provides the assessment tools, tools, and templates to get started. BCG suggests the following steps to take AI to scale in the organization in order to drive real value from their investments in artificial intelligence: (1) build an AI scale roadmap, (2) organize for success with an AI at scale organization, and (3) implement AI at scale.

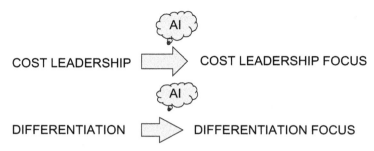

Figure 2 Cost leadership and differentiation transformation through AI

Companies that pioneer the application of AI to their business processes are rapidly transforming not only their own operations, but their whole sector. We see examples in healthcare and the pharmaceutical sector that increasingly relies on prediction. Instead of serving people through offering therapies for their existing health issues, it starts offering possibilities of avoiding diseases through data analytics. This shift will lead to the redefinition of what "focus-oriented cost leadership" and "focus-oriented differentiation" mean in the context of health and wellness offerings. Other market players, who decide to join this next level of digital and cognitive transformation, may indeed join too late. Laggers and experimenters who stop at the level of introducing one or two inconclusive pilot projects will not take AI to scale and reap its benefits. Yet, the pioneers are risking enormous resources for uncertain gains.

As of now, AI is streamlining companies to more constrained strategic choices of available tools and solutions and a sharper focus on a competitive advantage (Birkinshaw 2020).

The key to differentiation is identifying and targeting the most valuable customers. These customers are not always the most active or the most loyal. They are, however, the ones that generate the most value for the company, and therefore, they should be the focus of the company's attention. This can be achieved using predictive methods, although regression or classification may not be enough (Reis et al. 2020).

Both companies pursuing cost leadership and those pursuing differentiation need a clear understanding of their customer base and what motivates their customers to buy their products or services (see Figure 2). Once the most valuable customers have been identified, companies need to create a differentiated experience for them. This may involve customizing the product or service offering, creating a unique customer service experience, or developing a loyalty program that rewards the most valuable customers. Differentiating the experience for the most valuable customers is not only about creating a better experience for them; it is also about creating a unique experience that cannot be easily replicated by competitors. This may require companies to rethink their business model and their go-to-market strategy. Companies that are able to identify and target their most valuable customers will be able to generate more revenue and profits than companies that cannot.

To summarize, AI is having a profound impact on the development and execution of strategy in organizations. Strategy has always been about making better decisions, and AI is giving organizations new ways to do this. AI can help organizations to identify patterns and trends in data, to make better predictions, and to identify new opportunities. Organizations are also using AI to automate tasks and free up resources that can be redirected to more strategic activities. For example, a retailer might use AI to automatically reorder stock when it reaches a certain level, or a bank might use AI to automatically flag suspicious activity on customer accounts. AI is also changing the way that organizations interact with customers. Companies are using AI-powered chatbots to handle customer queries, and they are using AI to personalize the customer experience. The impact of AI on strategy is likely to increase in the future as the technology continues to develop. Organizations that are not already using AI in their strategy process should begin to explore how it can be used to improve their decision-making.

7 The Rise of Natural Language Understanding in Business: Case of Marketing

TL;DR GPT summary: We explore how NLP can be used in marketing, specifically in the context of content generation and customer segmentation. We will see how NLP can be used to generate targeted content for specific customer segments, and how it can be used to automatically segment customers based on their language usage.

Natural language processing and understanding – respectively, NLP (Manning et al. 2014; Hirschberg and Manning 2015) and NLU (Allen 1988; Liu et al. 2019) – are fields at the intersection of AI, computer science, and linguistics that deal with the interactions between computers and human (natural) language, specifically the task of programming computers to process and analyze large amounts of linguistic data – mostly natural text (Manning and Schutze 1999; Manning et al. 2014). Both NLP and NLU can accurately extract information and insights contained in documents, as well as categorize and organize the documents themselves, segment thematically the content they contain, et cetera. Natural language processing challenges often involve speech recognition, natural language understanding, and natural language generation. The goal of NLP and NLU is to create a system capable of contextually "understanding" the content of documents, including the nuances of the language in them, and to converse freely with humans. This is undoubtedly one of the most dynamically developing disciplines of AI, with a huge potential for application in business, education, public administration, or medicine. At the same time, it is a field in which the no-code and low-code approach is developing very fast, giving a chance to people from different professions (for example, marketers and content creators, as well as market analysts) to quickly implement conversational AI. This can be seen especially in the example of applications for the use of so-called transformers, which are described in more detail later in this section. In addition, the subfields of development of language processing and understanding, and their corresponding algorithms, which will certainly increase in the coming years, are presented in a tabular form: from rule-based and AI chatbots (Gupta, Hathwar, and Vijayakumar n.d.), through recurrent networks and word embeddings, to the aforementioned language transformers, which constitute a kind of revolution in NLP and NLU.

In text analysis, including handwriting recognition (Plamondon and Srihari 2000), and language processing in general, as well as human speech synthesis, the use of machine-learning algorithms called recurrent neural networks has been very popular in recent years. Recurrent neural networks (RNNs) are a class of networks in which connections between nodes form a directed graph along a temporal sequence (Mikolov et al. 2010). This allows them to exhibit dynamic behavior over time, and this is very important when working with language. The key idea of recurrent neural networks is precisely the use of sequential information. In a traditional neural network, we assume that all inputs (and outputs) are independent of each other, but in language processing this approach will not work. For example, in order to predict the next word in a sentence, it is better to know which words came before it. Recurrent neural networks get their name from the fact that they perform the same task for every element in the sequence, and the output always depends on the previous computation. We can also think of RNNs as having a "memory" that captures information about what has been computed so far and takes it into account in subsequent computations (Mnih et al. 2013). These networks are used for various time series analyses (e.g., stock prices), among other applications, but most notably they have become popular in the broad field of natural language processing, including automatic translation, text-to-speech solutions, and sentiment analysis.

Of particular note in the context of RNNs are Long Short-Term Memory (LSTM) networks, invented by Hochreiter and Schmidhuber (1997), which have set accuracy records in many application areas, mainly in speech prediction and sentiment analysis. Around 2007, LSTMs began to revolutionize speech recognition, outperforming traditional models in some speech applications. In 2009, the Connectionist Temporal Classification or CTC-trained LSTM network was the first RNN to win speech pattern recognition competitions when it won several competitions in connected handwriting recognition. LSTM also improved speech recognition with an extensive, rich vocabulary and has been successfully used in Google's Android system, among others. Also, LSTM networks have broken records in improved machine translation. Moreover, together with convolutional networks (CNN), LSTM networks have improved automatic image signing. A particular example of an LSTM network is the gated recurrent unit (GRU) cell (Cho et al. 2014), a simplified version of LSTM very often used in text analysis.

Encoder–decoder networks are increasingly being used to work with natural language. At the beginning, machine translation was an important area of development, but these networks are already used for text generation, including creative work such as generating marketing leads or blog title proposals, as well as in conversations with people. More and more often in the latter role, they replace classic chatbots.

There are at least several text generators based on encoder–decoder architecture called transformers. These include BERT (Zhao, Li, and Lu 2018), T-5 (Karita et al. 2019), GPT-3 (Fröhling and Zubiaga 2021; Elkins and Chun 2020), DALL-E (Durall et al. 2021), and Google's Meena transformer currently under development. There will undoubtedly be more transformers in the future due to their scalability and broad application potential. For instance, GPT-3 (or Generative Pre-trained Transformer 3) is an autoregressive language model that uses deep learning to create human-like text. It is the third generation predictive model in the GPT-n series (and successor to the equally famous GPT-2) created by one of the most pioneering companies in the AI field, OpenAI. The full version of GPT-3 has a capacity of 175 billion machine-learning parameters. Released in May 2020 and in beta testing as of July 2020, GPT-3 is part of the trend of NLP and NLU systems relying on pre-trained language representations. Prior to the release of GPT-3, the largest language model was Microsoft's Turing NLG, introduced in February 2020, with a capacity of 17 billion parameters – less than one-tenth the capacity of GPT-3.

The quality of text generated by GPT-3 is so high that it can be difficult to determine whether it was written by a human, which has both benefits and risks. Thirty-one OpenAI researchers and engineers presented the original May 28, 2020, paper introducing GPT-3. In their paper, in addition to showing the many advantages of the system, capable of more than just high-context text analysis, conversation, or music composition, they warned of the potential dangers of GPT-3. David Chalmers, an Australian philosopher, described GPT-3 as one of the most interesting and important AI systems ever produced. GPT-3 has been trained on hundreds of billions of words and is capable of coding in CSS, JSX, Python, among others. In addition to GPT-3, there is also GPT-J, an open-source version of the transformer released in 2021, and being extended all the time, as well as extremely popular ChatGPT.

The majority of transformers share the property of text generation – they are able to create text from data. This, by the way, can be done using a variety of methods, including NLP and machine learning, but systems like GPT far exceed other more traditional methods. Moreover, transformers often rely on model completion as the process of filling in missing values in a data set. This can be done using a variety of methods, including imputation and interpolation. GPT is a machine-learning platform that enables developers to train and deploy AI models. It is also said to be scalable and efficient with the ability to handle large amounts of data. It can be used for a variety of tasks, including text generation, model completion, and data analysis. Some examples of using GPT-3 in marketing include: generating targeted marketing content, developing marketing strategies, identifying potential customers, and analyzing customer behavior.

T5, is a type of text-to-text transformer that can be trained for various tasks with a unified architecture, while Dall-E (Singh, Deng, and Ahn 2021) is an AI program that creates images from text descriptions, revealed by OpenAI on January 5, 2021. It uses a version of the GPT-3 transform model to interpret natural language input and generate corresponding images.

Bidirectional Encoder Representations from Transformer (BERT), on the other hand, is the first of the transformers and, in this sense, a technically groundbreaking model for NLP (Devlin et al. 2018) which was built by the Google AI team. It is not uncommon for Google to emphasize the importance of BERT for contextual language understanding when analyzing page content and or queries. A pre-trained platform, BERT, while still in beta, produced very interesting results in processing eleven assigned language tasks. These tasks included semantic role labeling, text classification, next sentence prediction, and so on. It was originally trained primarily on the English-language Wikipedia. Polish language equivalents of the BERT network, based on this transformer, are the RoBERT Large and HerBERT models created by the Information Processing Center.

For the purpose of this section, we have selected marketing. Marketing is one of the primary components of business management and commerce (Harvard Business Review and Silk 2006) and as such comprises activities, processes, and institutions dedicated to designing, communicating, delivering, and exchanging offerings that have value for customers, partners, and clients, as well as society at large. Marketing is very internally broad as a type of knowledge work, and requires, among other things, creativity, but at the same time it produces measurable outcomes. Therefore, in the context of many other management tasks and practices, it presents itself as both promising and challenging in terms of AI implementation. What is more, many marketing-oriented activities are suitable material for training to the most advanced state-of the-art AI algorithms in general, and conversational AI in particular. Conversational bots are a particular type of software designed to help human white-collar workers (professional, desk, managerial, or administrative work). Using advanced NLP, multi-layer neural networks, and vast knowledge bases techniques, they can make sense out of unstructured data, build their knowledge base, and perform selected, usually narrowly defined tasks. Users communicate with such bots by using either chat or voice commands.

All transformers are already proving to be very useful as support for marketing tasks (generating keywords and blog titles, as well as leads for marketing campaigns in social media) and content creation in the broad sense (poems, stories, essays, simple journalistic forms, and posts for social media), sentiment analysis in the context of users' perception of services and products, 24/7 conversation with customers, customer service, product recommendations, matching visuals to keywords, and even creating musical compositions. In the future, the range of their applications will undoubtedly expand, and with simplified, user-friendly interfaces (such as GPT-3 and AI 21 Labs already have) that do not require coding, many professionals in different industries will be able to use them successfully (Floridi and Chiriatti 2020; Branwen 2020; Zhang, Bengio et al. 2021). One of the latest developments in language and speech understanding is also the Chinese Wu Dao system. In June 2021, Beijing Academy of Artificial Intelligence (BAAI) launched Wu Dao 2.0, the successor to Wu Dao 1.0. Wu Dao is a language model that aims to outperform OpenAI's GPT-3 or Google's LaMDA (another powerful transformer) in operating language at the human level. Wu Dao is trained on 4.9 terabytes of images and text.

Let us look more carefully at GPT. Among the functionalities that are most important for this research, we can enumerate: (1) chat, (2) product name generator, (3) spreadsheet generator, (4) TL;DR generator, (5) analogy maker, (6) essay outline, and (7) ad from product description. We see GPT-3 (Fröhling and Zubiaga 2021; McGuffie and Newhouse 2020) is an autoregressive language model that uses deep learning to produce, among other things, human-like text or code. The applicant has already acquired access to the API of the GPT model, which will allow for development of an almost professional level chatbot that will be fine-tuned to help study participants in performing their specific tasks. Recently, the GPT-3 model has been successfully used in similar tasks (Elkins and Chun 2020; Thiergart, Huber, and Übellacker 2021). Let us analyze the example below (see Figure 3):

After fine-tuning (see Figure 4) that is, making the prompt more precise and providing target audience as well as specific course or program, these are the results obtained:

Write a creative ad for the following product to run on Facebook:

Product: Kozminski University

Kozminski University is one of the best business schools in Europe! offer a world-class education that will prepare you for a successful career in business. Our faculty is comprised of experienced professionals who are passionate about teaching. We offer a variety of programs that will meet your needs and help you achieve your goals. Contact us today to learn more about our programs and how we can help you reach your potential!

Figure 3 Prompt for GPT-3

Write a creative ad for the following product to run on Facebook aimed at business people: |product: Kozminski University's executive MBA program

Are you looking for an executive MBA program that will help you take your career to the next level? Look no further than Kozminski University! Our world-class faculty will prepare you for a successful future in business. We offer a variety of programs that are tailored to meet your needs and help you achieve your goals. Contact us today to learn more about our programs and how we can help you reach your potential!

Write a creative ad for the following product to run on Facebook aimed at millennials: Product: Kozminski University's "Artificial Intelligence in Business" BA program

Are you looking for a program that will prepare you for a career in the exciting field of artificial intelligence? Look no further than Kozminski University's "Artificial Intelligence in Business" BA program! Our experienced faculty will provide you with the skills and knowledge you need to succeed in this rapidly growing field. Contact us today to learn more about our program and how we can help you reach your potential!

Figure 4 Fine-tuned prompt for GPT-3

Here GPT-3 and other transformers are models trained by billions of data, designed to act in an unsupervised way, displaying a high degree of context awareness. As we have just seen with this example, it is also possible to fine-tune them in order to capture what we want to express.

In business terms, it means getting rid of a cumbersome process of training the model on huge data sets. Also, there are ways of using, developing, and fine-tuning transformers with a very easy-to-use low-code library called huggingface.co. We will expand on this topic in the following sections, but what we can say already now is that whereas today we mostly use advanced programming frameworks like PyTorch and Tensorflow in order to work with transformers, huggingface.co is a herald of change in terms of accessibility: a simple no-barrier interface to deal with transformers.

Using all the frameworks, including the low-code ones, we can do spectacular things with transformers, like training it to run sentiment analysis, having it perform

Name Entity Recognition (NER) by exactly identifying the entities described in a text (a capability for all chatbots talking to clients), generating personalized text, answering client questions, summarization (like TL;DR which we have used for section abstracts in this Element), translation, and text comparison.

Summarizing, we can say with great certainty that transformers bring about change in the analysis of unstructured textual data and through that redefine the competitive edge. They will reshape providing services to customers via virtual assistants, rapid sentiment analysis, and data visualization. They will profoundly redefine customer experience platforms and customer experience management.

8 Democratizing and Anti-competitive Aspects of AI

TL;DR GPT summary: In this section we focus on democratizing AI. In business strategy, the dawn of AI technologies has accelerated the "coopetitive" phenomena: on the one hand, unique data sets and the first-mover's advantage are even more important, and yet on the other cooperating with direct competition is often the fastest way to secure them.

Fun fact: An article titled "Is AI Going Mainstream at Last?" was written in 1998. Although the answer was far from clear, the sense of urgency and lack of patience was clearly palpable more than two decades ago (Hedberg 1998). Alas, it has taken more than twenty years since that publication for AI to truly go mainstream by any definable measures. As we have observed in the previous sections, AI is definitely more and more widespread across different sectors and enterprise functions. AI "mainstream," however, can mean different things. It be understood both as a broad penetration of different organizational functions, different sectors, and tackling different kinds of data and as opening new levels of usability through less technically demanding tools and applications (low-code and no-code) (Luo et al. 2021)

Low-code, no-code tools (Shaikh 2020) and approach to AI are designed to simplify the process of creating software applications, making it possible for people with little or no coding experience to build them. The hope is that the removal of barriers of app development can lead to the creation of more innovative and useful applications, and offer access to more people than ever (Kobayashi, Ishibashi, and Kobayashi 2019).

Simplification can also be seen in the way these tools make it easier to deploy and manage applications. For instance, they often include features that automate the process of setting up and maintaining a development or test environment. This can save significant time and effort, particularly for larger applications. Low-code, no-code tools can also help to reduce the cost of developing and deploying applications. By simplifying the process and making it possible for more people to get involved, they can help to reduce the need for still-scarce specialists such as developers and testers. Although there is a huge demand for AI technologies, there are very few AI experts. Thus, low-code, no-code platforms are often promoted as being "democratizers," making it possible for anyone to create an app without any coding experience.

Most of the barriers to using AI were related to the difficulties of mastering formal language and the time needed to do that. The cumbersome path from programming, coding to data science and data analytics, and further on to machine learning and deep learning seemed like a story with no happy ending. This effectively prevented AI from going mainstream and becoming a general purpose technology like the Internet (Ciechanowski et al. 2018)

A low-code platform enables developers to create code quickly and easily using a graphical user interface (GUI). This type of software can be used to develop applications that are simple to understand and implement. Due to the ease of use of low-code platforms, developers can create simple and effective software applications without having to write complex code. They can also use a visual editor to draw flowcharts.

Today, there are several low-code platforms used by developers and non-programmers, among which are Mendix, Outsystems, and Appian. By making the development of software applications easier, a wider audience can use these tools. Such easy-to-use low-code platformsare used in developing software applications for industries such as the Internet of Things (IoT), edge computing, and AI.

Developers can use no-code software to create full-featured apps without having to learn programming. They can simply drag and drop software elements into the application using a visual development interface.

No-code AI tools, which include platforms with functionalities of Cloud AutoML, Cloud AutoML Tables, Cloud AutoML Video Intelligence, Cloud AutoML Vision, and Cloud AutoML Natural Language, enable you to train and deploy machine learning models without writing code. These tools allow to train models using users' own data and then use those models to automatically label images, videos, and text. The users can also train models that identify objects, faces, and landmarks in images, and models that transcribe speech in video and audio files. Other no code tools are Akkio (end-to-end no-code AI platform designed for sales, marketing, and financial activities); Runway (for creators who want to turn their visuals and data into AI fodder without coding); and Google AutoML (a suite of AI products that enables you to train high-quality machine-learning models tailored to your unique business needs). Amazon SageMaker or Lobe are free desktop programs created by Microsoft to help users build customized AI models simply by clicking.

However, not all low-code, no-code platforms are equally easy to use. Some require more technical expertise than others, and some may be more suitable for certain types of applications. It is therefore important to select a platform that is right for the task.

Despite a consensus that simplification of AI usage and reduction of barriers are beneficial, there are several issues at stake when it comes to defining AI democratization. Even the most advanced AI systems can be tainted by errors and biases. This is because developers who are not experts can introduce these issues into the system. This could leave companies with a huge amount of work to do to protect their systems. It's also important to avoid getting caught up in the hype over AI.

So, what does it take to democratize AI? It takes data, vendors, privacy, and respect for values.

Accessibility of data, and the ability to reduce the noise within that data are important components of making AI a go-to business technology. There are different types of problems regarding data. On one hand, too much data does not always generate significant business insights; on the other, many small and medium-sized companies complain of lack of access to qualitative data. There is a difference between big and smart data and multiple small data sets that are not actionable. There is certainly no definition of "good data," as it can depend on the context and what is being analyzed. In general, good data is accurate, complete, and timely. It is also of high quality, free from errors, inconsistencies, and biases (Cai and Zhu 2015; Loshin 2010; Pipino, Lee, and Wang 2002).

Andrew Ng (Strickland 2022) argues for "unbiggening" AI. In Section 7, we demonstrated transformers, powerful foundational language models that serve not only as text generators, translators, or bridges between formal and natural language, but also as predictive tools. Such models do not need that much data to learn anymore, so there is less need to collect huge volumes of data. Moreover, as Ng argues, in many industries giant datasets don't exist, so the focus has to shift from big data to quality data. "Having 50 thoughtfully engineered examples can be sufficient to explain to the neural network what you want it to learn." This will allow for a paradigm shift. As we already mentioned, data-centric. AI uses data to drive decision-making. It works on data quality to build an AI system. Whereas the prioritized paradigm over the last decade was to improve the code, attention is now on the data itself. Data-centric AI has a great potential in marketing, healthcare, and finance (Faulkner and Nicholson 2020; Malinowski and Zimányi n.d.).

The second thing that we need to democratize AI is vendors. They determine which parts of their platform or tools will be democratized. One end of the spectrum is data, which is the material that enables organizations to generate value from their data. As the data is fed into the algorithms, the complexity and value of the data increases. This transition is easy to achieve with open-source code repository sites such as GitHub.

Even with an AI-capable system, people still need a basic understanding of math and computer science to implement its algorithms. Over the past five years, the evolution of the technology platform has allowed users to access and train deep learning models on a pay-as-you-go basis.

Unlike algorithms, cloud-based platforms don't require deep learning training or certification. Instead, users can develop their own models that they can then use to solve specific problems.

The emergence of tools and platforms that allow users to develop automated machine-learning models has democratized model development. For instance, users can now run multiple algorithms on the same data set.

Unfortunately, many people are not trained to implement deep learning models – and here we enter another dimension of AI's accessibility. Too much access can be a problem too. It could lead to the development of biased algorithms and make it hard to explain the results of the model. The risk of systemic abuse of models increases as organizations collect more data. Having this knowledge is important to avoid making the most of AI.

Are we trying to open AI for the casual users or are we going to democratize it for the power users? This is a very difficult question. Democratizing should be done with caution and care to avoid fraud, abuse, and bias. Leaders should also take action. Training is one of the most critical factors that organizations should consider when developing and implementing AI models. Not having this training could have disastrous effects on the development and operations of AI systems. Microsoft (Bisser 2021; Masood and Hashmi 2019) already claims to have democratized the entire data science process by creating drag-and-drop tools.

While it's important to have the right people in place to implement AI, they should also have the knowledge and skills to design, test, and maintain the system. An example is when a business user created a machine learning model using a tool that was widely available. The model was over-optimized to the data set and its results could have been inaccurate. As a result, the organization lost money due to the flaws in the model. Most of the time, casual users don't have the training to develop and implement effective models. This is usually why many companies choose to work with experienced developers or data scientists. This should, however, by no means deter the use of low-code approaches. Ultimately, they are a gateway to a complex but promising technology with incredible potential if it's used on a large scale. What we wish to underline is that low-code on its own is certainly not enough. Democratization should not equal easy access to potential misuse. No-code deep-fake platforms where everyone whose picture is available online can be turned into a porn star is not democratizing. Low-code requires awareness, best practices, but also regulations (like the upcoming EU "AI Act"[4]). If the goal is to democratize AI, users should be trained to use it safely. Leaders should also consider the ownership of the data that they collect using AI tools. When data is collected for an AI or machine-learning program, it should be kept secure and not used for other applications. This ensures that the data is being used only for the intended purpose.

Nonetheless, some parts of the process can be safely democratized. For instance, when it comes to democratized data visualization, we tend to focus on the low-risk proposition of letting people create their own models instead of relying on specialist data scientists.

The third component of democratization of AI is privacy and respect of values. We should certainly avoid shadow AI, that is, AI applications collecting and using data without the proper permissions or oversight from the organization. Establishing a robust data governance system is also necessary to minimize risks and keep the data secure. A good data governance system should ensure that the models are developed according to the right validation and success metrics. It should also prevent the models from being deployed without being able to explain their results.

On the horizon, we see several interesting and viable solutions. One of these is federated learning – a technique for training machine-learning models on data that is distributed across cell phones or sensors. Devices train a shared model independently and then share their updates with each other. The updates are aggregated to produce a new global model (Kairouz et al. 2021; Konečný et al. 2016). Another is the emerging trend of privacy computing, a new field that uses technology to protect user data from unauthorized access or disclosure. This can include everything from developing secure software to designing hardware that is resistant to tampering (Li et al. 2016)

There have also been many descriptions of homomorphic encryption: encryption algorithms designed to allow mathematical operations to be performed on encrypted data without first decrypting it (Axelsson and Khrennikov 2019; Fan and Vercauteren 2012).

Yet another challenge to democratization pertains to intellectual property (IP). The perceived benefits of democratized data are only achieved if the parties are able to agree on who owns the IP rights for the data. Many companies are reluctant to use cloud platforms due to concerns that their sensitive information will be leaked. A critical step in the entire process of democratized data is to establish an open-sourcing agreement. Doing so

---

[4] "Laying Down Harmonized Rules on Artificial Intelligence (Artificial Intelligence Act) and Amending Certain Union Legislative Acts" https://eur-lex.europa.eu/legal-content/EN/TXT/?qid=1623335154975&uri=CELEX%3A52021PC0206.

should ensure that the parties do not violate any privacy or competitive dynamics. Through the discussion of the possible downsides of AI, organizations can explore the necessary standards and guidelines to ensure that their initiatives are successful.

Finally, it's not only about being data-centric, but human-centric. Certain "technological honesty," showing both the potential and challenges related to emerging tech is probably the best way to raise "citizen developer" within the organization and beyond it. "Citizen developers" are crucial for the trajectory of tech development in the future. They are non-technical developers who stand at the forefront of digital transformation. They may use no-code or low-code platforms to create simple automations for themselves, their teams and departments. They may have roles in HR, finance, sales and marketing, legal, procurement, and other business functions. They are not a substitute for a company's IT team, but they are indispensable in creating smaller automations that require a deeper understanding of individual tasks and departmental processes.

Around 40 percent of tasks can only be automated when you allow employees to drive demand. To reach the full potential of automation, citizen developers will amplify and evangelize automation. In many cases, automations created by citizen developers for a particular team are found to have greater use across the organization. To achieve this, organizations will need to invest in education and training. Some companies even run bot-a-thons to encourage employees to create their own robots, (robotic process automation) RPA-based solutions, and IoT applications. Others are offering self-selected upskilling courses, or their employees are taking advantage of online training in robotic process automation.

9 Collaborative AI

TL;DR GPT summary: Many techniques, such as natural language processing, can be implemented without coding. We are going to focus on the low-hanging fruit from the point of view of organizational strategy and technological development, and suggest practical ways of building up the AI muscle.

Many organizational leaders struggle with accurate mapping of AI's impact on their workforce and the speed of automation within their sector. That is because the question of AI's impact on the job market is immensely complex. Even though the public has been told that AI is taking people's jobs away, the real picture is much more nuanced. What we do know is that AI cannot replace most human workers. It will, nonetheless, lead to significant reskilling, generate new jobs and render some obsolete. Some researchers (Acemoglu and Restrepo 2017) claim that the rise of AI and robots has led to a reduction in employment and wages, suggesting the need for welfare systems to adopt "universal basic income" (UBI).

In addition, other authors claim that millions of jobs will be lost due to the rapid emergence of automated systems (Furman and Seamans 2019; Goolsbee 2018).

In a recent report, the Organization for Economic Co-operation and Development (OECD) AI Policy Observatory predicted that AI, together with IoT, Blockchain, and 5 G will create more jobs than they will eliminate. The report pointed out that companies that are pioneering the development and scaling of AI have so far not eliminated jobs on the net. According to the OECD AI Policy Observatory, there is no indication that this trend will not continue for the foreseeable future. A report by Stanford University's Human-Centered Artificial Intelligence on the transformation of work in the post-Covid era is in a similar vein. This makes it all the more worthwhile to invest in digital skills that enable more effective use of emerging technologies.

Nonetheless, the doomsday scenario of a jobless future – even if highly improbable – should incentivize researchers and governments to come up with normative approaches of AI's development that would best protect against adverse effects of automation for humans. "Collaborative AI" (cAI) is an interesting way forward in this direction that takes into account the possibility of building AI-based tools that automate tasks while working under human supervision. Collaborative AI is a relatively new response to the challenges of AI development and deployment. Its central idea is that AI should be developed and deployed in a way that is collaborative and inclusive of all stakeholders. We see two parallel discourses in the future of work: (1) automation of work leading to the replacement of humans:[5] and (2) cobotization, focusing on close collaboration with assistive technologies, especially AI.[6]

Significant advances in AI, deep learning, NLU, signal processing, and real-time IoT-driven data analysis, as well as machine vision, have led to the emergence of new human-centered collaborative systems (Haenlein and Kaplan 2019). Systems such as AlphaStar, AlphaGo (Vinyals et al. 2019; Wang et al. 2019), OpenAI Five (OpenAI 2018), and IBM Watson (Swan 2012) have proven that, in many cases, human–machine exchange should not be considered as competition and/or substitution, but rather as an area of potential collaboration where human talents can be augmented with machine computational intelligence.

---

[5] Automation of work that includes (1) fixed automation, (2) programmable automation, and (3) flexible automation. It can be caused by robots or RPA software in addition to AI: www.britannica.com/technology/automation/Manufacturing-applications-of-automation-and-robotics.

[6] Threats to jobs posed by AI and similar technologies can be assessed by examining core skill sets, that is, by distinguishing between durable jobs, those that will require reskilling, and those that will become obsolete (Latham and Humberd 2018). Some jobs that were durable during previous periods of business and technological shifts will remain durable in the foreseeable future, as will others, at least in the short- and medium-term perspective. Some workers will need significant reskilling but for others reskilling will be relatively minor.

As a rule, collaboration takes place between biological beings, but it leaves room for technology. In fact, collaboration between humans and machines can take many forms (Jemielniak and Przegalińska 2020). For instance, various tools designed and used for communication have long allowed for remote contact (immensely popular video conferencing tools, or other emerging technologies enabling telepresence, such as AR/ VR), but they have also become intermediaries of collaboration, allowing for collaborative, remote, and often asynchronous work (Slack and other messengers).

In the psychological literature (Conoley and Conoley 2010), collaboration is defined as "the act or process of two or more people cooperating toward a shared goal or an interpersonal relationship," in which each party is sensitive to the needs of the other.

As David Autor (2015) notes, machines both substitute for and complement human labor. Substituting for workers in routine tasks amplifies the comparative advantage of workers in terms of their problem-solving skills. Focusing on lost jobs misses the point that technology increases "the value of the tasks that workers uniquely supply." Automation has mostly affected routine and low-skilled tasks. For instance, the initial wave of industrial robots primarily affected manufacturing processes. AI's problem solving, reasoning, and perception capabilities mean that it can perform some non-routine cognitive tasks, like summarizing computer science research papers (Cachola et al. 2020). Recent evidence shows that companies are already increasing their productivity by using software robots to perform routine, rules-based service processes. If implemented well, such automation can result in high-performing human–robot teams, in which software robots and human employees complement one another. In some cases, automation does substitute for labor (Autor and Salomons 2018), but it also complements labor in many ways, raising output sufficiently to create higher demand for labor, and interacts with adjustments in labor supply, say, by increasing familial income enough to induce a spouse to leave the labor force.

Moreover, AI and automated tools will usually replace tasks, not jobs. A key insight is that a job can be viewed as a bundle of tasks, some of which offer better applications for technology than others (Autor, Levy, and Murnane 2000). Thus, particularly in the short term, researchers should think in terms of task replacement rather than unemployment. Some high-skilled professionals such as engineers, radiologists, or lawyers are at risk because most of the tasks they perform can be done by AI. Such highly educated professionals, however, may also be capable of applying AI in a way that complements their work.

We are now entering the next level of human–technology collaboration. This happens when a system can create synergistic effects with humans: generating added value that would not exist if such collaboration did not occur. A proponent of the collaborative approach to emerging technologies such as IoT and AI, moreover, is Tom Malone of the MIT Sloan School of Management – whose work is mentioned in this Element and who, in *Superminds* (Malone 2018), argues for the power of humans and machines working and thinking together. He also argues that advances in AI can allow for the emergence of novel ideas and even solutions to the most pressing problems. It is worth mentioning that the convergence of human and robot capabilities is often discussed as a possible solution to the dystopian scenario in which AI will annihilate humanity as postulated by many prominent futurologists.

According to Malone, AI should develop domain knowledge rather quickly, becoming expert in specific tasks. Equipped with such AI, humans would use their own talents, abilities, and skills (including knowledge synthesis) more effectively to solve problems (Malone 2018). For example, an experimental study showed that productivity can be enhanced (Manyinka et al. 2017; Seamans and Raj 2018) when developing an assembly system for human–robot collaboration. More such examples can be found: for example, systems that support creative work (generative AI for music composition or screenwriting writing or drafting marketing campaigns), and intelligent systems used in factories. Malone (2018) advocates for the power of humans and machines working and thinking together. Malone argues that advances in AI and connectivity could generate novel ideas, and, by inducing collective intelligence, solutions to the most pressing problems could be discovered.

Malone distinguishes several models of collaboration between machines and humans. We can talk about parallel work or independent work, we can talk about working on several "sections" of one task or project, but we can also talk about interdependence, such as when the decision made by a tech-system (e.g., in medical diagnostics where patient data retrieved from sensors is cross-pollinated with historical data) is a support for the doctor, who then verifies it. The most desirable and, according to Malone, achievable system would be full cooperation with AI, giving synergy effects. In such a variant, a human uses those dimensions of intelligence in which he or she is the best, and his or her cognitive and decision-making horizon is supported by advanced, albeit specialized, AI.

Taking all this into account, there are several levels of use and corresponding technical skills. The first of these will be basic skills in the use of tools and interfaces that do not require coding corresponding to the "product" approach to IoT and AI. Any person proficient in social media or applications will be able to use AI in this area, as is already evident from marketers using transformative solutions such as the AI21 Labs, or Facebook users using the simple Chatfuel platform to build chatbots that can be transferred to IoT devices.

Second will be the level where you already know basic coding (for example, Python or Javascript) and machine-learning algorithms, including NLP algorithms, which allows you to apply ML and NLP in various problem spaces. Here you can use ready-made platforms to build and optimize IoT and AI tools, choose the best algorithms for a problem.

The penultimate stage will be advanced skills in NLU programming, which allows you to use all libraries and tools, including deep learning, to implement projects using AI. The final stage will be the creation of AI tools and conversational AI from scratch, and having extensive knowledge and experience in deep learning algorithms and reinforcement learning.

As we have argued in Section 6, in the retail industry, AI is being used to create more personalized shopping experiences for customers and to help retailers better understand customer behavior. In the financial industry, AI is being used to help banks and financial institutions more accurately assess risk and detect fraud. The question is, however, how to carefully craft AI with different degrees of proximity to human expertise and to truly put "human in the loop" and design interfaces that are both easy to use and exciting for human workers. The spectrum of digital skills summarizes possible trajectories of reskilling. Reskilling is the process of learning new skills or acquiring new knowledge to perform a different job or tasks other than the ones you are currently performing (Illanes et al. 2018; Newman and Winston 2016).

What about the other side of the equation? What about machines becoming more intuitive and easier to use, and becoming more complementary to human knowledge and abilities needed at the workplace? Humans are being reskilled, but what about AI? Can its design allow it to reskill too, in order to work with diverse humans according to their pace and preferences? Can we create systems that are responsive to human needs? Certainly, there is no single collaborative solution. A big challenge that lies ahead for managers, CTOs, and AI officers is to figure out bottom-up approaches to reskilling and co-work with AI. Fruitful collaboration with AI is certainly not about generic AI tools. AI is an adaptive technology with great potential for personalization and this potential should be put to work. Employees' well-being and productivity both need to be taken into consideration while selecting tools and training pathways for individuals whose work can be enhanced by AI.

Many experts and organizations, including Partnership on AI, an industry-led consortium that includes major tech firms such as Google, Facebook, IBM, and Microsoft, have been advocating for collaborative AI over the past few years. The main reasons for supporting this direction of AI's development are related to the increasing complexity of AI and the associated risks, as well as the fact that activities related to AI are concentrated in a small number of large tech firms, which raises concerns about concentration of power and control. Last but not least, AI is increasingly being used for decision-making in areas such as healthcare, finance, and law, which raises the concerns about fairness, accountability, and transparency that we signaled in the previous section.

The goal of collaborative AI is to address these concerns by promoting the development and deployment of AI in a way that is open, inclusive, and transparent. Collaborative AI is still in its early stages, and it is not yet clear how it will be implemented. The concept has the potential to transform the way AI is developed and used, and to improve the accountability, fairness, and transparency of AI systems.

10 The Day after Tomorrow

TL;DR GPT summary: AI is evolving and its future is uncertain. We don't know what will happen but it is possible that AI will become more intelligent than humans and change the world in ways we cannot predict.

The future of AI is shrouded in potential and fraught with uncertainty. Most often, when any casual talk about AI begins, it almost immediately turns into a utopian or dystopian scenario-building exercise that has little to do with machine learning or deep learning. More often than not, singularity pops up as the main topic of the conversation that washes off any interest in AI as we already know it, and that will most likely stay with us for a couple of decades. The reason we fall into all the speculation is obvious: the future of AI is notoriously difficult to predict. Perhaps AI will eventually surpass human intelligence, or perhaps AI will remain subordinate to humans. Highly unsatisfying conclusion, but thankfully we do not have to stop here.

To discuss AI's future, let's first analyze its past. The history of AI can be divided into a number of stages, each of which has its own level of development and application:

(1) Prehistory (before the 1950s). AI was proposed as a field of study. AI research was largely theoretical and focused on logic, problem solving, and knowledge representation.
(2) Foundational period (1950s–70s). This period saw the development of key AI technologies such as artificial neural networks, expert systems, and robotics.
(3) Applied period (1980s–2020s). AI research centers on developing applications. This period has seen the development of machine learning, natural language processing, and computer vision.
(4) Future period (2020s-onwards) AI is expected to achieve human-level intelligence. This period will see the development of technologies such as artificial general intelligence and whole brain emulation.

Since the 1950s, fluctuations in interest in AI have affected the pace of its development.[7] The term "AI winter" (Floridi 2020; Lloyd 1995; Umbrello 2021) is often used to describe a period of reduced funding and research interest in AI. It is analogous to a "nuclear winter" in which nuclear war causes global cooling. The first AI winter is believed to have occurred between 1974 and 1980. It was caused by several factors, including the withdrawal of government funding in the United States and the UK, and the collapse of the Lisp Machine market (Hendler 2008). The second AI winter occurred in the early 1990s. This has caused the failure of expert systems to live up to their hype, the collapse of the early artificial neural network market, and slow progress in robotics (Toosi et al. 2021).

Later, the discipline moved on, strangely strengthened by the two crises. Several advancements were made and, around 2010, deep neural networks, combined with sufficient computational power and huge volumes of data produced the AI boom (Qin 2020).

The question of the AI season has boomeranged on us. We may narrow down the question to the one that is focused on the next decade. What to expect in the coming years? Is the next AI winter on the horizon? Is the concept of AI winter historically justified? Many experts debate whether we have AI springtime or AI summer, taking into account the deployment of AI across the economy. However, there is no precise answer.

We probably won't see another AI winter (see Figure 5). This is because AI is already being deployed in many functional areas within enterprises and organizations, and it has already demonstrated encouraging results. There is no reason to believe that deep neural networks will go away anytime soon, as they are already being used to train massive models. However, the fascination with AI does not really match its general performance yet. Moreover, the discipline is still not yet well-defined, and this may have caused people to exaggerate its potential.

Several projects that caught the attention of tech investors and the public have failed. For instance, I do not think that self-driving cars will be ready soon. In terms of AR/VR, Magic Leap has laid off many employees, and Google has also reduced its focus on this technology. It may, however, come back with a recent push toward Metaverse (Duan et al. 2021; Sparkes 2021). However, in the past couple of years, companies such as Amazon, Facebook, and Google started hiring more people through AI residency programs. Most technology companies have also made significant investments in the development of AI.

---

[7] Whereas some authors perceive AI winters severely hindered the progress of AI, some others claim their impact was rather marginal.

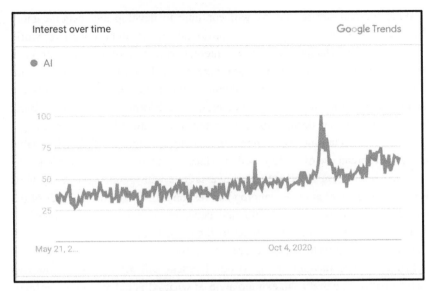

Figure 5 Google Trends for AI

These companies have established large AI labs that can serve as a hub for academic and industrial research. These labs can also release large-scale data-sets and provide high-quality code.

Some experts trying to predict what is next for AI point to strictly technological problems and shortcomings (Iansiti and Lakhani 2020). Various technical challenges were revealed when the research world collided with the real world. AI in general (and deep learning in particular), is a capricious technology: when deployed it may lead to significant cost reductions for some sectors, but in others it has not become the promised change maker. Regarding new revenue streams thanks to AI, we have not seen much evidence of that either. Despite this, continued investment from both the industry and the research community will still help overcome these issues. However, civil society will need to be included (and not just bypassed) in order to ensure that the systems are ethical and safe.

Also, let's take into account that conditions today are more robust than the uncontrolled and unjustified hype of the late twentieth century. The rise of the Internet laid the foundation for a culture of open research and development. We have learned from the past. Having realistic expectations is very important when it comes to AI. We should not expect another AI winter due to the disillusionment that happened in the past. AI technology will continue to be widely used. Despite the huge need for AI expertise, the world has enough experts to handle it. This could affect how special AI experts feel compared to other fields.

What we can say is that AI will continue to develop and become more important in our lives. It will have a profound impact on how we live, work, and play. It will change the way we interact with technology and with each other. It will transform how we learn, how we heal, and how we manage our environment. Despite the many unknowns about the future, AI experts are optimistic about the technology's potential to transform our lives in profound ways in the years and decades to come. In the near future, AI will continue to get better at understanding and responding to natural language. This will enable more widespread use of voice-based interfaces, and will make it possible for AI systems to carry on more natural conversations with people. As AI systems become more adept at understanding and responding to the complexities of the world, they will be used to automate decision-making in a wide range of domains. This will free up humans to focus on higher-level tasks, and will enable organizations to operate more efficiently.

In the short to medium term, AI development will most likely follow two distinct paths. The first is an extrapolation of what AI is today – highly special-ized, deep learning algorithms applicable to clearly defined problems in a more complex, contextual, and nuanced way. The second path involves creating AI systems capable of processing information in a manner similar to the human brain. Today, deep neural networks have become a key paradigm in AI due in part to an algorithm called backpropagation (Hecht-Nielsen 1992; Schrittwieser et al. 2020). They are also the ones that make best use of real-time data collected from sensors and the Internet of Everything. This backpropagation enables deep neural networks to learn from data and thus achieve capabilities such as language translation, speech recognition, and image classification – again here, data from IoT is key. Narrowly specialized AI is unlikely to affect the number of jobs per se, but like previous technological revolutions, it will cause a profound shift in the economy and redefine the tasks facing workers, transform business models and strategies, and the ways in which institutions operate.

The second path of biologically inspired AI requires IoT and real-time data. It has great potential to transform the capabilities of AI and overcome its current limitations, creating more robust and complex systems capable of more abstract levels of reasoning. However, it is many years away (McAfee and Brynjolfsson 2016; McAfee and Brynjolfsson 2017;Tegmark 2017) and it is difficult – at least for now – to speculate on how it will change the labor market and how it will affect the relationship between humans and technology.

AI could enable us to extend our cognitive abilities in ways that are difficult to imagine. For example, we might develop AI-assisted methods for enhancing our memory or for learning new skills more quickly. Alternatively, we might use AI to help us better understand and control our emotions. Ultimately, the future of artificial intelligence will be determined by the choices we make as a society about how to develop and use this powerful technology.

Artificial intelligence will also rely on relationships with other powerful technologies, like IoT, blockchain, and VR. AI's future trajectories will depend on how fruitful these intersections become. There is, however, one more discipline in which potential overlap with AI could bring spectacular, but challenging, outcomes: synthetic biology.

Have you heard of xenobots? They are small, biological robots made from frog cells. They are designed to perform specific tasks and can be used for medical purposes, such as delivering drugs to specific parts of the body or cleaning up radioactive material (Coghlan and Leins 2020; Ramanujam et al. 2022).

Xenobots are less than a millimeter in size and composed of 500–1000 skin and heart cells from African frog (*Xenopus laevis*) embryos at the blastula stage. After culturing extracted embryonic stem cells, microsurgery tools help "glue" the sticky cells together in a range of simple organismic configurations, or "novel lifeforms" (Kriegman et al. 2020). By then, the stem cells have become skin cells, which provide scaffolding, and heart cells, which spontaneously contract, giving the xenobots locomotion. "Their design determines their autonomous functional capacities, which include being able, *in aqua*, to move linearly or circularly, swarm, 'explore,' push small objects, and hold objects in a pouch" (Kriegman et al. 2020).

Prior to biological assembly, *in silica* design models are generated by a supercomputer with deep neural networks. Primed with relevant biophysical principles, the evolutionary algorithm predicts which of innumerable possible cellular configurations will produce desired functions, and *"in vivo* testing results can then be looped back into the algorithm to generate new bespoke design models" (Kriegman et al. 2020).

Looking back at two-year progress of xenobots, and simultaneously looking into the next two or three decades with AI, we may expect, with moderate probability, some forms of "artificial life" (Thompson 2014; West 2018) like the "xenobots" that few people have heard of, but that – as a form of applied technology – have gravity comparable with cloning. Ethical consideration of what the future holds if such forms of artificial life actually came to life are beyond the scope of this Element. It is, however, important to have them in mind. It certainly transgresses any considerations regarding AI seasons we have been conducting thus far.

We conclude with a small anecdote. While writing this section we asked GPT-3 to tell us a bit about the AI winter. GPT-3 told us "The third AI winter is believed to have begun around 2007, caused by the failure of commercial applications of artificial intelligence to meet expectations." Well, if this is the winter, let's brace ourselves for the summer, because it may reveal itself as such a technological acceleration that we will need enhanced seat belts to survive it.

Conclusions

In the Element, we explored how artificial intelligence can be used in organizations and beyond. We placed special attention on tectonic shifts in business strategies due to AI's implementation. We discussed the potential benefits and risks of AI, and provided insights into how businesses can use AI to create value. We have also included case studies of companies that have successfully used AI in their business strategy.

Along the way, we examined the collaborative potential of AI.

An image often associated with collaboration in the workplace is when employees work together to complete a task or reach goals. They accomplish this through brainstorming, discussion, and sharing of ideas. We believe that all that can also be done with and through AI, and that this very perspective on AI may prove to be equally important and efficient for businesses as AI-enabled optimization or prediction.

Today, there is no single answer to this question, as it depends on the specific application or project. However, in general, collaboration with AI refers to working with AI-powered tools and systems to complete tasks or achieve goals. This can involve training and developing AI models, working with AI to carry out tasks, or using AI to improve human decision-making.

While writing this Element, we did our best to use the power of AI for ideation and writing. We allowed AI to take over minor, carefully selected tasks. For instance, we have generated some of the section titles with AI21 Lab's "generate catchy headlines" functionality and outlined section structure with "blog post ideation" functionality. Section abstracts were generated with GPT-3's TL;DR functionality. In the first section, we used GPT-3's fine-tuned spreadsheet generator to generate examples of AI algorithms' applications. You will also find small portions of highlighted text in each section. Throughout this journey of working together with AI the following discovery emerged as most prominent: the power of AI needs proper guidance and competences – it will not do much on its own.

Like other language transformers, for example, the AI21 Labs, GPT-3 has a very accessible no-code interface that allows non-experts to use it for research and business purposes. The barrier of formal language is lifted, but simple delegation of tasks won't do. Let's have a look at the example of books that,

Table 3 "10 books about artificial intelligence and business strategy
(1st prompt)" by GPT-3

10 books about artificial intelligence and business strategy (1st prompt)
1   *Competing on Analytics: The New Science of Winning* (Frederiksen 2009)
2   *The Innovator's Dilemma: When New Technologies Cause Great Firms to Fail* (Christensen 2013)
3   *The Halo Effect: How Managers Let Themselves Be Deceived* (Rosenzweig 2008)
4   *The Wisdom of Crowds* (Goldstein, McAfee, and Suri 2014)
5   *The Black Swan: The Impact of the Highly Improbable* (Taleb 2007)
6   *Blink: The Power of Thinking without Thinking* (Gladwell 2006)
7   *Freakonomics: A Rogue Economist Explores the Hidden Side of Everything* (Azar 2006)
8   *SuperFreakonomics: Global Cooling, Patriotic Prostitutes, and Why Suicide Bombers Should Buy Life Insurance* (Pinheiro 2011)
9   *The Signal and the Noise: Why So Many Predictions Fail – But Some Don't* (Draper 2013)
10   *Moneyball: The Art of Winning an Unfair Game* (Lewis 2004)

according to the foundational language model GPT-3, talk about AI in business strategy (Table 3) We have not trained the model on this task and the results rely fully on the search that the model performed without any fine-tuning:

When we analyze these selections, we see at once that some of the books can be considered as interesting choices in terms of "business" or "economics," but the majority are really peripheral to "AI for business strategy." We can safely assume that the model performed a search for the most popular books and bestsellers in the sphere of economics while neglecting "AI."

This is because GPT-3 has been pre-trained on a vast amount of text from the open Internet. When given a prompt with no examples, it relies on generic and usually suboptimal searches. However, with just a few examples, it can often sense what task you are trying to perform and generate a plausible completion. This is often called "few-shot learning." Fine-tuning improves on few-shot learning by training on many more examples than can fit in the prompt, letting the users achieve better results on a larger number of tasks. Once we prepared and uploaded training data (a list prepared in natural language that contained books we considered relevant), we trained the fine-tuned model and used it to generate another list (Table 4). This saved cost and enabled lower-latency requests.

Table 4 "10 books about artificial intelligence and business strategy
(2nd prompt)" by GPT-3

**10 books about artificial intelligence and business strategy
(2nd prompt – after fine-tuning)**

1   *Lean AI: How Innovative Startups Use Artificial Intelligence to Grow* by
    Lomit Patel (Patel 2020)
2   *Artificial Intelligence for Business: Understand Neural Networks and
    Machine Learning for Robotics. A Step-by-Step Method to Develop AI
    and ML Projects for Business* by David Brown (Brown 2020)
3   *AI for Business Leaders: How to Harness the Power of Artificial
    Intelligence to Grow Your Business* by Paul Daugherty and H. James
    Wilson
4   *The Future of Work: How the New Order of Business Will Shape Your
    Organization, Your Management Style, and Your Life* by Thomas
    W. Malone (Gantman 2005)
5   *The Second Machine Age: Work, Progress, and Prosperity in a Time of
    Brilliant Technologies* by Erik Brynjolfsson and Andrew McAfee
    (Brynjolfsson and McAfee 2014)
6   *The Lean AI Organization* by Paul Miller
7   *The AI Advantage* by Thomas H. Davenport (Davenport 2018)
8   *Data Strategy: How to Profit from a World of Big Data, Analytics and
    Artificial Intelligence* by Bernard Marr (Marr 2021)
9   *The Second Machine Age: Work, Progress, and Prosperity in a Time of
    Brilliant Technologies* by Erik Brynjolfsson and Andrew McAfee
    (Brynjolfsson and McAfee 2014)
10 *Machine, Platform, Crowd: Harnessing Our Digital Future* by Andrew
    McAfee and Erik Brynjolfsson (McAfee and Brynjolfsson 2017)

Now, please have a look at the list after it was fine-tuned:

After fine-tuning, we certainly obtained much better results in relation to strategy and AI. Two of the books, however, do not exist: *The Lean AI Organization* by Paul Miller and *AI for Business Leaders: How to Harness the Power of Artificial Intelligence to Grow Your Business*" by Paul Daugherty and H. James Wilson. Paul Miller is the practice vice-president of Garnter and publishes in the area of AI. There is a book called *Lean AI* by Lomit Patel, listed among the books recommended. Paul Daughtery and James Wilson wrote the intriguing *Human + Machine* (2018) that does match our criteria. More attempts at fine-tuning generated slightly better results in terms of choices, but crossing out made-up books turned out to be impossible using fine-tuning methods.

Does AI need supervision?

No, AI does not need supervision.

This is not correct.

AI definitely needs supervision, as it is not yet advanced enough to make decisions on its own. It still requires humans to provide it with guidance and direction, in order to avoid making mistakes.

Figure 6 Conversation with GPT-3

We would have to set up rules in the terminal to prevent the system from listing the made-up titles.

Toward the end of our writing, we asked GPT-3 whether or not human supervision is necessary for AI. The first answer was " AI needs no supervision." We disagreed. Then, the system responded, "AI definitely needs supervision, as it is not yet advanced enough to make decisions on its own. It still requires humans to provide it with guidance and direction, in order to avoid making mistakes."

Correct, GPT-3: we would have written this book without AI, but AI would not have written it without us.

Thus, what AI also needs, and what we humans excel at, is collaboration with other humans, not just today, but also in the future (Figure 6). And now let us leave you with some handpicked readings we are comfortable recommending (and yes, we can also be biased):

Agrawal, Ajay, Joshua Gans, and Avi Goldfarb. 2018. *Prediction Machines: The Simple Economics of Artificial Intelligence*. Brighton, MA: Harvard Business Press.

Dörfler, Victor. 2022. *What Every CEO Should Know About AI*. Cambridge: Cambridge University Press.

Iansiti, Marco, and Karim R. Lakhani. 2020. *Competing in the Age of AI: Strategy and Leadership When Algorithms and Networks Run the World*. Harvard Business Press.

Jemielniak, Dariusz. 2020. *Thick Big Data*. Oxford: Oxford University Press.

Jemielniak, Dariusz and Aleksandra Przegalinska. 2020. *Collaborative Society*. Cambridge, MA: MIT Press.

Malone, T. W. 2018. *Superminds: The Surprising Power of People and Computers Thinking Together*. New York: Little Brown.

A picture generated by OpenAI's DALL·E 2 algorithm on 2022-07-22 with a prompt: "A black-and-white, super-realistic, and detailed drawing of two androids fighting on a chessboard with katanas."

References

Acemoglu, Daron, and Pascual Restrepo 2017. "Robots and Jobs: Evidence from US Labor Markets." https://doi.org/10.3386/w23285.

Acemoglu, Daron, and Pascual Restrepo. 2018. "Artificial Intelligence, Automation and Work." Working Paper Series. National Bureau of Economic Research. https://doi.org/10.3386/w24196.

Allen, James. 1988. *Natural Language Understanding*. San Francisco: Benjamin-Cummings Publishing.

Amit, Raphael, and Christoph Zott. 2020. *Business Model Innovation Strategy: Transformational Concepts and Tools for Entrepreneurial Leaders*. New York: John Wiley & Sons.

Amsalem, Orly. 2022. "Five Ways to Shift to AI-First." Datanami. 2022. www.datanami.com/2022/02/22/five-ways-to-shift-to-ai-first/.

Anadiotis, George. 2022. "Andrew Ng Predicts the Next 10 Years in AI." *VentureBeat*. March 21, 2022. https://venturebeat.com/2022/03/21/andrew-ng-predicts-the-next-10-years-in-ai/.

Autor, David H. 2015. "Why Are There Still So Many Jobs? The History and Future of Workplace Automation." *The Journal of Economic Perspectives: A Journal of the American Economic Association* 29 (3): 3–30.

Autor, David, and Anna Salomons. 2018. "Is Automation Labor-Displacing? Productivity Growth, Employment, and the Labor Share." No. 24871. National Bureau of Economic Research. https://doi.org/10.3386/w24871.

Autor, David, Frank Levy, and Richard Murnane. 2000. "Upstairs, Downstairs: Computer-Skill Complementarity and Computer-Labor Substitution on Two Floors of a Large Bank." NBER working paper. https://doi.org/10.3386/w7890.

Axelsson, Ekaterina Yurova, and Andrei Khrennikov. 2019. "Description of (Fully) Homomorphic Cryptographic Primitives Within the P-Adic Model of Encryption." *Trends in Mathematics*. https://doi.org/10.1007/978-3-030-04459-6_23.

Azar, Ofer H. 2006. "Freakonomics: A Rogue Economist Explores the Hidden Side of Everything." *The Economic Journal* 116 (512): F335–36.

Banker, Sachin, and Salil Khetani. 2019. "Algorithm Overdependence: How the Use of Algorithmic Recommendation Systems Can Increase Risks to Consumer Well-Being." *Journal of Public Policy & Marketing* 38 (4): 500–15.

Barrat, James. 2013. *Our Final Invention: Artificial Intelligence and the End of the Human Era*. London: Macmillan.

Bean, Randy. 2021. "NewVantage Partners Releases 2021 Big Data and AI Executive Survey." www.businesswire.com/news/home/20210104005022/en/NewVantage-Partners-Releases-2021-Big-Data-and-AI-Executive-Survey.

Beduschi, Ana. 2021. "Rethinking Digital Identity for Post-COVID-19 Societies: Data Privacy and Human Rights Considerations." *Data & Policy* 3. https://doi.org/10.1017/dap.2021.15.

Behm, Carly. 2022. "As Neuralink Aims for Human Trials, 3 Spine Surgeons Weigh in on Practicality." *Becker's Orthopedic & Spine Review.* January 13, 2022. www.beckersspine.com/spine/item/53404-as-neuralink-aims-for-human-trials-3-spine-surgeons-weigh-in-on-practicality.html.

Benkler, Yochai, Robert Faris, and Hal Roberts. 2018. *Network Propaganda: Manipulation, Disinformation, and Radicalization in American Politics.* Oxford: Oxford University Press.

Birkinshaw, Julian. 2020. "What Is the Value of Firms in an AI World?" In *The Future of Management in an AI World*, 23–35 Canais, Jordi; Heumcamp Franz. Cham: Springer International Publishing.

Bisser, Stephan. 2021. "Introduction to the Microsoft Conversational AI Platform." *Microsoft Conversational AI Platform for Developers.* https://doi.org/10.1007/978-1-4842-6837-7_1.

Bogen, Miranda. 2019. "All the Ways Hiring Algorithms Can Introduce Bias." *Harvard Business Review*, May 6, 2019. https://hbr.org/2019/05/all-the-ways-hiring-algorithms-can-introduce-bias

Bory, L. 2019. "Deep New: The Shifting Narratives of Artificial Intelligence from Deep Blue to AlphaGo." *Convergence: The International Journal of Research into New Media Technologies*, 25 (4). https://doi.org/10.1177/1354856519829679.

Bostrom, Nick. 2015. *Superintelligence: Paths, Dangers, Strategies*, vol. 66. Oxford: Oxford University Press.

Branwen, Gwern. 2020. "GPT-3 Creative Fiction," June. www.gwern.net/GPT–3.

Brooks, Rodney. 2017. "The Seven Deadly Sins of AI Predictions." *MIT Technology Review*, October 6, 2017. www.technologyreview.com/2017/10/06/241837/the-seven-deadly-sins-of-ai-predictions/.

Brown, David. 2020. *Artificial Intelligence for Business: Understand Neural Networks and Machine Learning for Robotics. A Step-By-Step Method to Develop AI and Ml Projects for Business.* London: 17 Books Limited.

Brynjolfsson, Erik, and Andrew McAfee. 2014. *The Second Machine Age: Work, Progress, and Prosperity in a Time of Brilliant Technologies.* New York: W. W. Norton & Company.

Bulusu, Lakshman, and Rosendo Abellera. 2020. *AI Meets BI: Artificial Intelligence and Business Intelligence*. Boca Ratan, FL: CRC Press.

Buolamwini, Joy Adowaa. 2017. "Gender Shades: Intersectional Phenotypic and Demographic Evaluation of Face Datasets and Gender Classifiers." Massachusetts Institute of Technology. https://dspace.mit.edu/handle/1721.1/114068?show=full.

Burkhardt, Marcus. 2019. "Mapping the Democratization of AI on GitHub." *The Democratization of Artificial Intelligence*. https://doi.org/10.14361/9783839447192-013.

Cachola, Isabel, Kyle Lo, Arman Cohan, and Daniel S. Weld. 2020. "TLDR: Extreme Summarization of Scientific Documents." *arXiv [cs.CL]*. arXiv. http://arxiv.org/abs/2004.15011.

Cai, Li, and Yangyong Zhu. 2015. "The Challenges of Data Quality and Data Quality Assessment in the Big Data Era." *Data Science Journal* 14 (0): 2.

Cho, Kyunghyun, Bart van Merrienboer, Caglar Gulcehre et al. 2014. "Learning Phrase Representations Using RNN Encoder-Decoder for Statistical Machine Translation." *arXiv [cs.CL]*. arXiv. http://arxiv.org/abs/1406.1078.

Christensen, Clayton M. 2013. *The Innovator's Dilemma: When New Technologies Cause Great Firms to Fail*. Boston, MA: Harvard Business Review Press.

Ciechanowski, Leon, Aleksandra Przegalinska, Mikolaj Magnuski, and Peter Gloor. 2018. "In the Shades of the Uncanny Valley: An Experimental Study of Human–chatbot Interaction." *Future Generations Computer Systems: FGCS*, February. https://doi.org/10.1016/j.future.2018.01.055.

Clifford, Cat. 2018. "Google CEO: A.I. Is More Important than Fire or Electricity." CNBC. February 1, 2018. www.cnbc.com/2018/02/01/google-ceo-sundar-pichai-ai-is-more-important-than-fire-electricity.html.

Coghlan, Simon, and Kobi Leins. 2020. "'Living Robots': Ethical Questions about Xenobots." *The American Journal of Bioethics: AJOB* 20 (5): W1–3.

Daugherty, Paul R., and H. James Wilson. 2018. *Human + Machine: Reimagining Work in the Age of AI*. Boston, MA: Harvard Business Review Press.

Davenport, Thomas H. 2018. "The AI Advantage." https://doi.org/10.7551/mitpress/11781.001.0001.

Davenport, Thomas H., and Rajeev Ronanki. 2018. "Artificial Intelligence for the Real World." *Harvard Business Review* 96 (1): 108–16.

David, Javier E. 2017. "Elon Musk Issues a Stark Warning about A.I., Calls It a Bigger Threat than North Korea." CNBC. August 12, 2017. www.cnbc.com/2017/08/11/elon-musk-issues-a-stark-warning-about-a-i-calls-it-a-bigger-threat-than-north-korea.html.

Dickson, Ben. 2020. "Sorry, Elon: Fully Autonomous Tesla Vehicles Will Not Happen Anytime Soon." PCMAG. July 16, 2020. www.pcmag.com/opinions/ sorry-elon-fully-autonomous-tesla-vehicles-will-not-happen-anytime-soon.

Domingos, Pedro. 2015. *The Master Algorithm: How the Quest for the Ultimate Learning Machine Will Remake Our World*. New York: Basic Books.

Domingos, Pedro, and Geoff Hulten. 2001. "A General Method for Scaling Up Machine Learning Algorithms and Its Application to Clustering." In *Proceedings of the Eighteenth International Conference on Machine Learning*, editing by Carla E. Brodley and Andrea Pohoreckyj Danyluk, eds. http://citeseerx.ist.psu.edu/viewdoc/summary?doi=10.1.1.21.2571.

Domonoske, Camila. 2017. "Elon Musk Warns Governors: Artificial Intelligence Poses 'Existential Risk.'" *NPR*, July 17, 2017. www.npr.org/ sections/thetwo-way/2017/07/17/537686649/elon-musk-warns-governors-artificial-intelligence-poses-existential-risk.

Draper, Norman R. 2013. "*The Signal and the Noise: Why So Many Predictions Fail – But Some Don't* by Nate Silver." *International Statistical Review*. https://doi.org/10.1111/insr.12020_24.

Duan, Haihan, Jiaye Li, Sizheng Fan et al. 2021. "Metaverse for Social Good: A University Campus Prototype." In *Proceedings of the 29th ACM International Conference on Multimedia*, 153–61. New York: Association for Computing Machinery.

Durall, Claudia, Kateryna Kukil, Jeffrey A. Hawkes et al. 2021. "Production of Succinate by Engineered Strains of Synechocystis PCC 6803 Overexpressing Phosphoenolpyruvate Carboxylase and a Glyoxylate Shunt." *Microbial Cell Factories* 20 (1): 39.

Elkins, Katherine, and Jon Chun. 2020. "Can GPT-3 Pass a Writer's Turing Test?" *Journal of Cultural Analytics*, September. https://doi.org/10.22148/ 001c.17212.

Fan, Junfeng, and Frederik Vercauteren. 2012. "Somewhat Practical Fully Homomorphic Encryption." *Cryptology ePrint Archive*. https://eprint.iacr .org/2012/144.

Faulkner, Alastair, and Mark Nicholson. 2020. "Data-Centric Systems." *Data-Centric Safety*. https://doi.org/10.1016/b978-0-12-820790-1.00018-8.

Floridi, Luciano. 2020. "AI and Its New Winter: From Myths to Realities." *Philosophy & Technology* 33 (1): 1–3.

Floridi, Luciano, and Massimo Chiriatti. 2020. "GPT-3: Its Nature, Scope, Limits, and Consequences." *Minds and Machines* 30 (4): 681–94.

Frank, Blair Hanley. 2017. "You Might Use AI, but That Doesn't Mean You're an AI Company." *VentureBeat*. September 19, 2017. https://venturebeat.com/ 2017/09/19/you-might-use-ai-but-this-doesnt-mean-youre-an-ai-company/.

Frederiksen, Anders. 2009. "Competing on Analytics: The New Science of Winning." *Total Quality Management & Business Excellence* 20 (5): 583–83.

Fröhling, Leon, and Arkaitz Zubiaga. 2021. "Feature-Based Detection of Automated Language Models: Tackling GPT-2, GPT-3 and Grover." *PeerJ. Computer Science* 7 (April): e443.

Furman, Jason, and Robert Seamans. 2019. "AI and the Economy." *Innovation Policy and the Economy* 19 (January): 161–91.

Gantman, Ernesto R. 2005. "Book Review: Thomas W. Malone, *The Future of Work: How the New Order of Business Will Shape Your Organization, Your Management Style, and Your Life*." *Organization Studies* 26 (8): 1258–63.

Girasa, Rosario. 2020. *Artificial Intelligence as a Disruptive Technology*. Cham: Palgrave.

Gladwell, Malcolm. 2006. "Blink: The Power of Thinking without Thinking." www.journalofadvertisingresearch.com/content/jadvertres/46/1/135.full-text.pdf.

Goldstein, Daniel G., Randolph Preston McAfee, and Siddharth Suri. 2014. "The Wisdom of Smaller, Smarter Crowds." In *Proceedings of the Fifteenth ACM Conference on Economics and Computation*, 471–88. EC '14. New York: ACM.

Good, Irving John. 1966. "Speculations Concerning the First Ultraintelligent Machine." In *Advances in Computers*, edited by Franz L. Alt and Morris Rubinoff, 6: 31–88. Elsevier.

Goolsbee, Austan. 2018. "Public Policy in an AI Economy." No. 24653. National Bureau of Economic Research. https://doi.org/10.3386/w24653.

Grand View Research. 2021. "Artificial Intelligence Market Size Analysis Report, 2021–2028." www.grandviewresearch.com/industry-analysis/artificial-intelligence-ai-market.

Gupta, Aishwarya, Divya Hathwar, and Anupama Vijayakumar. n.d. "Introduction to AI Chatbots." *International Journal of Engineering Research & Technology* (IJERT), 9 (7) July. https://pdfs.semanticscholar.org/f5f4/746acffef08df37f184cb6acc0505362ea9b.pdf.

Haenlein, Michael, and Andreas Kaplan. 2019. "A Brief History of Artificial Intelligence: On the Past, Present, and Future of Artificial Intelligence." *California Management Review.* https://doi.org/10.1177/0008125619864925.

Harvard Business Review, and Alvin J. Silk. 2006. *What Is Marketing?* Boston, MA: Harvard Business Review Press.

Hecht-Nielsen, Robert. 1992. "Theory of the Backpropagation Neural Network." In *Neural Networks for Perception*, 65–93. Amsterdam: Elsevier.

Hedberg, S. R. 1998. "Is AI Going Mainstream at Last? A Look inside Microsoft Research." *IEEE Intelligent Systems and Their Applications* 13 (2): 21–25.

Hendler, James. 2008. "Avoiding Another AI Winter." *IEEE Intelligent Systems* 23 (2): 2–4.

Hermann, Erik. 2021. "Artificial Intelligence and Mass Personalization of Communication content: An Ethical and Literacy Perspective." *New Media & Society* 24 (5) June. https://doi.org/10.1177/14614448211022702.

Hildt, Elisabeth. 2019. "Artificial Intelligence: Does Consciousness Matter?" *Frontiers in Psychology* 10 (July): 1535.

Hirschberg, Julia, and Christopher D. Manning. 2015. "Advances in Natural Language Processing." *Science* 349 (6245): 261–66.

Hochreiter, S., and J. Schmidhuber. 1997. "Long Short-Term Memory." *Neural Computation* 9 (8): 1735–80.

Iansiti, Marco, and Karim R. Lakhani. 2020. *Competing in the Age of AI: Strategy and Leadership When Algorithms and Networks Run the World.* Boston, MA: Harvard Business Review Press.

Illanes, Pablo, Susan Lund, Mona Mourshed, Scott Rutherford, and Magnus Tyreman. 2018. "Retraining and Reskilling Workers in the Age of Automation." *McKinsey Global Institute.* www.echs-nm.com/wp-content/uploads/2019/10/retraining-and-reskilling-workers-in-the-age-of-automation-_-mckinsey-company.pdf.

Islami, Xhavit, Marija Topuzovska Latkovikj, Ljubomir Drakulevski, and Mirjana Borota Popovska. 2020. "Does Differentiation Strategy Model Matter? Designation of Oganizational Performance Using Differentiation Strategy Instruments: An Empirical Analysis." *Business: Theory and Practice.* https://doi.org/10.3846/btp.2020.11648.

Jemielniak, Dariusz. 2012. *The New Knowledge Workers.* Cheltenham: Edward Elgar.

Jemielniak, Dariusz. 2020. *Thick Big Data: Doing Digital Social Sciences.* Oxford: Oxford University Press.

Jemielniak, D., and Y. Krempovych. 2021. "An Analysis of AstraZeneca COVID-19 Vaccine Misinformation and Fear Mongering on Twitter." *Public Health* 200 (August): 4–6.

Jemielniak, Dariusz and Aleksandra Przegalinska. 2020. *Collaborative Society.* Cambridge, MA: MIT Press

Johnson, Stephen. 2022. "The Turing Test: AI Still Hasn't Passed the 'Imitation Game.'" *Big Think.* March 7, 2022. https://bigthink.com/the-future/turing-test-imitation-game/.

Kairouz, Peter, H. Brendan McMahan, Brendan Avent et al. 2021. "Advances and Open Problems in Federated Learning." *Foundations and Trends® in Machine Learning* 14 (1–2): 1–210.

Kak, Subhash. 2019. "Why a Computer Will Never Be Truly Conscious." *The Conversation*, October 16, 2019. http://theconversation.com/why-a-computer-will-never-be-truly-conscious–120644.

Kaltheuner, Frederike. 2021. *Fake AI*. New York: Meatspace Press.

Karita, Shigeki, Nanxin Chen, Tomoki Hayashi et al. 2019. "A Comparative Study on Transformer vs RNN in Speech Applications." In *2019 IEEE Automatic Speech Recognition and Understanding Workshop (ASRU)*, 449–56.

Kiron, David, and Michael Schrage. 2019. "Strategy for and with AI." *MIT Sloan Management Review*, June. https://sloanreview.mit.edu/article/strategy-for-and-with-ai/.

Kirsch, Noah. 2022. "Experts Are Ringing Alarms about Elon Musk's Brain Implants." *The Daily Beast*. January 25, 2022. www.thedailybeast.com/elon-musks-neuralink-inches-closer-to-human-trials-and-experts-are-ringing-alarms.

Kobayashi, Yasuyuki, Maki Ishibashi, and Hitomi Kobayashi. 2019. "How Will 'democratization of Artificial Intelligence' Change the Future of Radiologists?" *Japanese Journal of Radiology* 37 (1): 9–14.

Kohli, Sonali. 2015. "Bill Gates Joins Elon Musk and Stephen Hawking in Saying Artificial Intelligence Is Scary." *Quartz*. January 29, 2015. https://qz.com/335768/bill-gates-joins-elon-musk-and-stephen-hawking-in-saying-artificial-intelligence-is-scary/.

Konečný, Jakub, H. Brendan McMahan, Felix X. Yu et al. 2016. "Federated Learning: Strategies for Improving Communication Efficiency." *arXiv [cs.LG]*. arXiv. http://arxiv.org/abs/1610.05492.

Kouroutakis, Antonios E. 2019. "EU Action Plan against Disinformation: Public Authorities, Platforms and the People." https://papers.ssrn.com/abstract=3472887.

Kriegman, Sam, Douglas Blackiston, Michael Levin, and Josh Bongard. 2020. "A Scalable Pipeline for Designing Reconfigurable Organisms." *Proceedings of the National Academy of Sciences of the United States of America* 117 (4): 1853–59.

Latham, Scott, and Beth Humberd. 2018. *Four Ways Jobs Will Respond to Automation: The Level of Threat to a Given Profession Depends on Two Factors, the Type of Value Provided and How It's Delivered*. MIT Sloan Management Review.

Le Roy, Frédéric, and Anne-Sophie Fernandez. 2015. "Managing Coopetitive Tensions at the Working-Group Level: The Rise of the Coopetitive Project Team." *British Journal of Management* 26 (4): 671–88.

Levesque, Hector J. 2014. "On Our Best Behaviour." *Artificial Intelligence* 212 (July): 27–35.

Levy, Frank. 2018. "Computers and Populism: Artificial Intelligence, Jobs, and Politics in the Near Term." *Oxford Review of Economic Policy* 34 (3): 393–417.

Lewis, Michael. 2004. *Moneyball: The Art of Winning an Unfair Game.* New York: W. W. Norton & Company.

Li, Deyi, Wen He, and Yike Guo. 2021. "Why AI Still Doesn't Have Consciousness?" *CAAI Transactions on Intelligence Technology* 6 (2): 175–79.

Li, Feng-Hua, L. I. Hui, J. I. A. Yan, Neng-Hai Yu, and Weng Jian. 2016. "Privacy Computing: Concept, Connotation and Its Research Trend." *Journal on Communications* 37 (4): 1.

Liu, Xiaodong, Pengcheng He, Weizhu Chen, and Jianfeng Gao. 2019. "Multi-Task Deep Neural Networks for Natural Language Understanding." *arXiv [cs.CL].* arXiv. http://arxiv.org/abs/1901.11504.

Lloyd, John W. 1995. "Surviving the AI Winter." In *Logic Programming: The 1995 International Symposium*, edited by John Lloyd, 33–47. Cambridge, MA: MIT Press.

Loshin, David. 2010. *The Practitioner's Guide to Data Quality Improvement.* Amsterdam: Elsevier.

Loureiro, Sandra Maria Correia, João Guerreiro, and Iis Tussyadiah. 2021. "Artificial Intelligence in Business: State of the Art and Future Research Agenda." *Journal of Business Research* 129 (May): 911–26.

Luce, Leanne. 2019. "Democratization and Impacts of AI." *Artificial Intelligence for Fashion.* https://doi.org/10.1007/978-1-4842-3931-5_12.

Luckerson, Victor. 2014. "5 Very Smart People Who Think Artificial Intelligence Could Bring the Apocalypse." *Time*, December 2, 2014. https://time.com/3614349/artificial-intelligence-singularity-stephen-hawking-elon-musk/.

Luo, Yajing, Peng Liang, Chong Wang, Mojtaba Shahin, and Jing Zhan. 2021. "Characteristics and Challenges of Low-Code Development: The Practitioners' Perspective." In *Proceedings of the 15th ACM / IEEE International Symposium on Empirical Software Engineering and Measurement (ESEM)*, edited by Filippo Lanubie, 1–11. ESEM '21 12. New York: Association for Computing Machinery.

Magretta, Joan. 2011. *Understanding Michael Porter: The Essential Guide to Competition and Strategy.* Boston, MA: Harvard Business Review Press.

Mahalingam, Sundar. 2017. "Why 'Bridge' a Cerebral Game That Even AI Can't Conquer Deserves More Attention." September 7, 2017. www.dailyo.in/variety/bridge-ai-card-game-chess-go-sport/story/1/19380.html.

Malinowski, Elzbieta, and Esteban Zimányi. n.d. *Advanced Data Warehouse Design.* Berlin: Springer.

Malmi, Eric, Pyry Takala, Hannu Toivonen, Tapani Raiko, and Aristides Gionis. 2015. "DopeLearning: A Computational Approach to Rap Lyrics Generation." *arXiv [cs.LG]*. arXiv. http://arxiv.org/abs/1505.04771.

Malone, Thomas W. 2018. *Superminds: The Surprising Power of People and Computers Thinking Together*. New York: Little Brown.

Manheim, Karl, and Lyric Kaplan. 2019. "Artificial Intelligence: Risks to Privacy and Democracy." *Yale Journal of Law & Technology* 21: 106+.

Manning, Christopher D., Mihai Surdeanu, John Bauer et al. 2014. "The Stanford CoreNLP Natural Language Processing Toolkit." In *Proceedings of 52nd Annual Meeting of the Association for Computational Linguistics: System Demonstrations*, 55–60.

Manyika, James, Michael Chui, Mehdi Miremadi et al . 2017. "A Future That Works: AI, Automation, Employment, and Productivity." *McKinsey Global Institute Research, Tech. Rep* 60: 1–135.

Marr, Bernard. 2021. *Data Strategy: How to Profit from a World of Big Data, Analytics and Artificial Intelligence*. London: Kogan Page Publishers.

Martin, Roger L. 2015. "There Are Still Only Two Ways to Compete." *Harvard Business Review*, April 21, 2015. https://hbr.org/2015/04/there-are-still-only-two-ways-to-compete.

Martinez, Emmanuel. 2021. "The Secret Bias Hidden in Mortgage-Approval Algorithms." *Associated Press*. August 25, 2021. https://apnews.com/article/lifestyle-technology-business-race-and-ethnicity-mortgages-2d3d40d5751f9 33a88c1e17063657586.

Masood, Adnan, and Adnan Hashmi. 2019. "Democratization of AI Using Cognitive Services." In *Cognitive Computing Recipes: Artificial Intelligence Solutions Using Microsoft Cognitive Services and TensorFlow*, edited by Adnan Masood and Adnan Hashmi, 1–17. Berkeley, CA: Apress.

Mauro, Gianluco, and Nicolo Valigi. 2020. *Zero to AI: A Non-Technical, Hype-Free Guide to Prospering in the AI Era*. New York: Simon and Schuster.

McAfee, Andrew, and Erik Brynjolfsson. 2016. "Human Work in the Robotic Future: Policy for the Age of Automation." *Foreign Affairs* 95 (4): 139–50.

McAfee, Andrew, and Erik Brynjolfsson. 2017. *Machine, Platform, Crowd: Harnessing Our Digital Future*. New York: W. W. Norton & Company.

McCarthy, J., Minsky, M., Rochester, N., Shannon, C. 1955. "A Proposal for the Dartmouth Summer Research Project on Artificial Intelligence." *AI Magazine* 27 (4) (2006).

McGuffie, Kris, and Alex Newhouse. 2020. "The Radicalization Risks of GPT-3 and Advanced Neural Language Models." *arXiv [cs.CY]*. arXiv. http://arxiv.org/abs/2009.06807.

Metz, Cade. 2015. "Facebook's Human-Powered Assistant May Just Supercharge AI." *WIRED*. August 26: 2015.

Metz, Cade, and Neal E. Boudette. 2021. "Inside Tesla as Elon Musk Pushed an Unflinching Vision for Self-Driving Cars." *The New York Times*, December 6, 2021. www.nytimes.com/2021/12/06/technology/tesla-autopilot-elon-musk.html.

Mikolov, Tomas, Martin Karafiát, Lukas Burget, Jan Cernocky, and Sanjeev Khudanpur. 2010. "Recurrent Neural Network Based Language Model." In *Interspeech* 2:1045–48.

Mnih, Volodymyr, Koray Kavukcuoglu, David Silver et al et al. 2013. "Playing Atari with Deep Reinforcement Learning." *arXiv [cs.LG]*. arXiv. http://arxiv.org/abs/1312.5602.

Mooney, Ann. 2007. "Core Competence, Distinctive Competence, and Competitive Advantage: What Is the Difference?" *Journal of Education for Business* 83 (2): 110–15.

Newborn, Monty. 2012. *Kasparov versus Deep Blue: Computer Chess Comes of Age*. Berlin: Springer Science & Business Media.

Newman, Katherine S., and Hella Winston. 2016. *Reskilling America: Learning to Labor in the Twenty-First Century*. New York: Henry Holt and Company.

Ng, Andrew. 2016. "What Artificial Intelligence Can and Can't Do Right Now." *Harvard Business Review* 9 (11). www.w-t-w.org/de/wp-content/uploads/2016/11/Andrew-Ng-What-AI-Can-and-Can%E2%80%99t-Do.pdf.

Niedermeyer, Edward. 2019. *Ludicrous: The Unvarnished Story of Tesla Motors*. Dallas, TX: BenBella Books.

Nightingale, Sophie J., and Hany Farid. 2022. "AI-Synthesized Faces Are Indistinguishable from Real Faces and More Trustworthy." *Proceedings of the National Academy of Sciences of the United States of America* 119 (8). https://doi.org/10.1073/pnas.2120481119.

Noy, Ilan, and Tomáš Uher. 2022. "Four New Horsemen of an Apocalypse? Solar Flares, Super-Volcanoes, Pandemics, and Artificial Intelligence." *Economics of Disasters and Climate Change*, January, 1–24.

Olson, P. 2019. "Nearly Half of All 'AI Startups' Are Cashing in on Hype." *Forbes.Com*. www.forbes.com/sites/parmyolson/2019/03/04/nearly-half-of-all-ai-startups-are-cashing-in-on-hype/?sh=6b25c1d6d022.

OpenAI, Artem. 2018. "OpenAI Five."

Oriesek, Daniel F., and Jan Oliver Schwarz. 2020. *Winning the Uncertainty Game: Turning Strategic Intent into Results with Wargaming*. Routledge.

Ozbay, Feyza Altunbey, and Bilal Alatas. 2020. "Fake News Detection within Online Social Media Using Supervised Artificial Intelligence Algorithms." *Physica A: Statistical Mechanics and Its Applications* 540 (February): 123174.

Patel, Lomit. 2020. *Lean AI: How Innovative Startups Use Artificial Intelligence to Grow*. Sebastopol, CA: O'Reilly Media.

Pellegrin-Boucher, Estelle, Frédéric Le Roy, and Călin Gurău. 2013. "Coopetitive Strategies in the ICT Sector: Typology and Stability." *Technology Analysis & Strategic Management* 25 (1): 71–89.

Pinheiro, Roberto. 2011. "SuperFreakonomics: Global Cooling, Patriotic Prostitutes, and Why Suicide Bombers Should Buy Life Insurance." *The Academy of Management Perspectives* 25 (2): 86–87.

Pinker, Steven. 2018. *Enlightenment Now: The Case for Reason, Science, Humanism, and Progress*. London: Penguin UK.

Pipino, Leo L., Yang W. Lee, and Richard Y. Wang. 2002. "Data Quality Assessment." *Communications of the ACM* 45 (4): 211–18.

PlainSite. 2021. "California DMV Tesla Robo-Taxi / FSD Notes." www.plain site.org/documents/28jcs0/california-dmv-tesla-robotaxi–fsd-notes/.

Plamondon, R., and S. N. Srihari. 2000. "Online and Off-Line Handwriting Recognition: A Comprehensive Survey." *IEEE Transactions on Pattern Analysis and Machine Intelligence* 22 (1): 63–84.

Polo, Edison Fernandes, and Wilson Weber. 2010. "Competitive Generic Strategies Evolution and the Importance of Michael E. Porter." *Revista de Gestão*. https://doi.org/10.5700/rege389.

Porter, Michael E. 1997. "Competitive Strategy." *Measuring Business Excellence* 1 (2): 12–17.

Porter, Michael E. 2001. "Strategy and the Internet." *Harvard Business Review* 79 (3) March: 63–78.

Porter, Michael E., and Michael Gibbs. 2001. "Strategy and the Internet." https://140.78.51.40/static/0855380/files/strategy%20and%20the%20internet .pdf.

Primack, Dan. 2018. "What Google Isn't Telling Us about Its AI Demo." *Axios*. May 17, 2018. www.axios.com/google-ai-demo-questions-9a57afad-9854-41da-b6e2-5e55b619283e.html.

Qin, Tao. 2020. "Deep Learning Basics." In *Dual Learning*, edited by Tao Qin, 25–46. Singapore: Springer Singapore.

Ramanujam, Elangovan, L. Rasikannan, P. A. Anandhalakshmi, and Nashwa Ahmad Kamal. 2022. "Xenobots: A Remarkable Combination of an Artificial Intelligence-Based Biological Living Robot." *International Journal of Sociotechnology and Knowledge Development (IJSKD)* 14 (1): 1–11.

Regalado, Antonio. 2020. "Elon Musk's Neuralink Is Neuroscience Theater." *MIT Technology Review*, August 30, 2020. www.technologyreview.com/2020/08/30/1007786/elon-musks-neuralink-demo-update-neuroscience-theater/.

Reis, Carolina, Pedro Ruivo, Tiago Oliveira, and Paulo Faroleiro. 2020. "Assessing the Drivers of Machine Learning Business Value." *Journal of Business Research* 117 (September): 232–43.

Romer, Keith. 2022. "How A.I. Conquered Poker." *New York Times*, January 18, 2022. www.nytimes.com/2022/01/18/magazine/ai-technology-poker.html.

Rosenzweig, Phil. 2008. *The Halo Effect: How Managers Let Themselves Be Deceived*. New York: Simon and Schuster.

Ruggeri, Armando, Rosa Di Salvo, Maria Fazio, Antonio Celesti, and Massimo Villari. 2021. "Blockchain-Based Strategy to Avoid Fake AI in eHealth Scenarios with Reinforcement Learning." In *2021 IEEE Symposium on Computers and Communications (ISCC),* 1–7.

Sadilek, Adam, Stephanie Caty, Lauren DiPrete et et al. 2018. "Machine-Learned Epidemiology: Real-Time Detection of Foodborne Illness at Scale." *NPJ Digital Medicine* 1 (November): 36.

SAE. 2021. "SAE Levels of Driving Automation™ Refined for Clarity and International Audience." 2021. www.sae.org/blog/sae-j3016-update.

Sanchez, Oscar. 2020. "The Role of Artificial Intelligence in Investment Decision Making: A Study of Senior Management Perceptions within Private Equity and Venture Capital Firms." Masters thesis, Dublin, National College of Ireland. http://norma.ncirl.ie/id/eprint/4801.

Schmelzer, Ron. 2020. "The Changing Venture Capital Investment Climate for AI." *Forbes Magazine*, August 9, 2020. www.forbes.com/sites/cognitive world/2020/08/09/the-changing-venture-capital-investment-climate-for-ai/.

Schmidt, Eric, and Jonathan Rosenberg. 2014. *How Google Works*. New York: Grand Central Publishing.

Schrittwieser, Julian, Ioannis Antonoglou, Thomas Hubert et al. 2020. "Mastering Atari, Go, Chess and Shogi by Planning with a Learned Model." *Nature* 588 (7839): 604–09.

Schwartz, Oscar. 2019. "In 2016, Microsoft's Racist Chatbot Revealed the Dangers of Online Conversation." *IEEE Spectrum*. November 25, 2019. https://spectrum.ieee.org/in-2016-microsofts-racist-chatbot-revealed-the-dangers-of-online-conversation.

Seamans, Robert, and Manav Raj. 2018. "AI, Labor, Productivity and the Need for Firm-Level Data." No. 24239. National Bureau of Economic Research. https://doi.org/10.3386/w24239.

Searle, John R. 1980. "Minds, Brains, and Programs." *The Behavioral and Brain Sciences* 3 (3): 417–24.

Shaikh, Kasam. 2020. "AI with Low Code." *Demystifying Azure AI*. https://doi .org/10.1007/978-1-4842-6219-1_5.

Simon, Herbert A., and Allen Newell. 1958. "Heuristic Problem Solving: The Next Advance in Operations Research." *Operations Research* 6 (1): 1–10.

Singh, Gautam, Fei Deng, and Sungjin Ahn. 2021. "Illiterate DALL-E Learns to Compose." https://openreview.net/pdf?id=h0OYV0We3oh.

Sisson, Melanie, Jennifer Spindel, Paul Scharre, and Vadim Kozyulin. 2020. *The Militarization of Artificial Intelligence*. United Nations: Stanley Center for Peace.

Soleymanzadeh, Raha, Mustafa Aljasim, Muhammad Waseem Qadeer, and Rasha Kashef. 2022. "Cyberattack and Fraud Detection Using Ensemble Stacking." *AI*. https://doi.org/10.3390/ai3010002.

Sparkes, Matthew. 2021. "What Is a Metaverse." *New Scientist* 251 (3348): 18.

Spender, J-C. 2014. *Business Strategy: Managing Uncertainty, Opportunity, and Enterprise*. Oxford: Oxford University Press.

Spinney, Laura. 2022. "Artificial Intelligence Beats Eight World Champions at Bridge." *Guardian*, March 29, 2022. www.theguardian.com/technology/2022/mar/29/artificial-intelligence-beats-eight-world-champions-at-bridge.

Strack, Rainer, Miguel Carrasco, Philipp Kolo et al. 2021. "The Future of Jobs in the Era of AI.*" Boston Consulting Group*. https://web-assets.bcg.com/f5/e7/9aa9f81a446198ac5402aaf97a87/bcg-the-future-of-jobs-in-the-era-of-ai-mar-2021-r-r.pdf.

Strickland, Eliza. 2022. "Andrew Ng: Unbiggen AI." *IEEE Spectrum*. https://spectrum.ieee.org/andrew-ng-data-centric-ai.

"Study: AI for Fraud Detection to Triple by 2021." n.d. Accessed April 5, 2022. https://doi.org/10.1287/lytx.2019.04.22n.

Sutskever, Ilya. 2022. "It May Be That Today's Large Neural Networks Are Slightly Conscious." Twitter. February 9, 2022. https://twitter.com/ilyasut/status/1491554478243258368?s=20&t=Peui3i2uXQZPlXYHPpMtgw.

Swan, Melanie. 2012. "Sensor Mania! The Internet of Things, Wearable Computing, Objective Metrics, and the Quantified Self 2.0." *Journal of Sensor and Actuator Networks* 1 (3): 217–53.

Taleb, Nassim Nicholas. 2007. *The Black Swan: The Impact of the Highly Improbable*. London: Random House.

Tegmark, Max. 2017. *Life 3.0: Being Human in the Age of Artificial Intelligence*. New York: Knopf Doubleday.

Tenenbaum, J. B., V. de Silva, and J. C. Langford. 2000. "A Global Geometric Framework for Nonlinear Dimensionality Reduction." *Science* 290 (5500): 2319–23.

Thiergart, Jonas, Stefan Huber, and Thomas Übellacker. 2021. "Understanding Emails and Drafting Responses: An Approach Using GPT-3." *arXiv [cs.AI]*. arXiv. http://arxiv.org/abs/2102.03062.

Thompson, Steven John. 2014. *Global Issues and Ethical Considerations in Human Enhancement Technologies.* Hershey, PA: IGI Global.

Thompson, Will, and Nicole Cacal. 2022. *What's Your AI Strategy? The Forbes Ignite Guide to Customer-Centric Artificial Intelligence.* London: Wiley.

Toosi, Amirhosein, Andrea G. Bottino, Babak Saboury, Eliot Siegel, and Arman Rahmim. 2021. "A Brief History of AI: How to Prevent Another Winter (A Critical Review)." *PET Clinics* 16 (4): 449–69.

Turing, A. M. 1950. "Computing Machinery and Intelligence." *Mind: A Quarterly Review of Psychology and Philosophy* LIX (236): 433–60.

Umbrello, Steven. 2021. "AI Winter." In *Encyclopedia of Artificial Intelligence: The Past, Present, and Future of AI,* edited by Michael Klein and Philip Frana, 7–8. Santa Barbara, CA: ABC-CLIO.

Ventures, M. M. C. 2019. "The State of AI 2019: Divergence." 2019. https://web.archive.org/web/20200622202809/https://mmc.vc/wp-content/uploads/2019/02/The-State-of-AI-2019-Divergence.pdf.

Vigliarolo, Brandon. 2022. "1,000-plus AI-Generated LinkedIn Faces Uncovered." *The Register.* March 28, 2022. www.theregister.com/2022/03/28/ai_fake_linkedin_faces/.

Vinyals, Oriol, Igor Babuschkin, Wojciech M. Czarnecki et al. 2019. "Grandmaster Level in StarCraft II Using Multi-Agent Reinforcement Learning." *Nature* 575 (7782): 350–54.

Wang, Dakuo, Justin D. Weisz, Michael Muller et al. 2019. "Human-AI Collaboration in Data Science: Exploring Data Scientists' Perceptions of Automated AI." *Proc. ACM Human-Computer Interaction,* 211, 3 (CSCW): 1–24.

West, Darrell M. 2018. *The Future of Work: Robots, AI, and Automation.* Washington, DC: Brookings Institution Press.

Williams, Al. 2017. "AI: This Decade's Worst Buzz Word." *Hackaday.* September 18, 2017. https://hackaday.com/2017/09/18/ai-this-decades-worst-buzz-word/.

Wischmeyer, Thomas, and Timo Rademacher, eds. 2020. *Regulating Artificial Intelligence.* Cham: Springer.

Wright, Robert E., and Aleksandra Przegalińska. 2021. "Universal Basic Income: How Crazy of an Idea Is It Really?" *AIER.* April 30, 2021. www.aier.org/article/universal-basic-income-how-crazy-of-an-idea-is-it-really/.

Zhang, Chiyuan, Samy Bengio, Moritz Hardt, Benjamin Recht, and Oriol Vinyals. 2021. "Understanding Deep Learning (Still) Requires Rethinking Generalization." *Communications of the ACM* 64 (3): 107–15.

Zhang, Yi, Mengjia Wu, George Yijun Tian, Guangquan Zhang, and Jie Lu. 2021. "Ethics and Privacy of Artificial Intelligence: Understandings from Bibliometrics." *Knowledge-Based Systems* 222 (June): 106994.

Zhao, Bin, Xuelong Li, and Xiaoqiang Lu. 2018. "HSA-RNN: Hierarchical Structure-Adaptive RNN for Video Summarization." *2018 IEEE/CVF Conference on Computer Vision and Pattern Recognition.* https://doi.org/10.1109/cvpr.2018.00773.

Cambridge Elements ≡

Business Strategy

J.-C. Spender
Kozminski University

J.-C. Spender is a research Professor, Kozminski University. He has been active in the business strategy field since 1971 and is the author or co-author of 7 books and numerous papers. His principal academic interest is in knowledge-based theories of the private sector firm, and managing them.

About the Series

Business strategy's reach is vast, and important too since wherever there is business activity there is strategizing. As a field, strategy has a long history from medieval and colonial times to today's developed and developing economies. This series offers a place for interesting and illuminating research including industry and corporate studies, strategizing in service industries, the arts, the public sector, and the new forms of Internet-based commerce. It also covers today's expanding gamut of analytic techniques.

Cambridge Elements ≡

Business Strategy

We propose a clear and up-to-date description of the state of artificial intelligence today, not only in terms of business processes and strategies, but also its societal reception. This Element presents our view of the technology landscape, avoiding both the forward-looking, rose-colored utopia and the hyper-apocalyptic gloom. It does so in a concise form, addressing a complex issue in nine concise and easy-to-read sections. Our aim is to discuss the current state of machine learning and AI in strategic management, and to describe the emerging technologies. We conceptualize their adoption, and then consider the effects of AI technologies' maturity in business organizations.

About the Series
Business strategy's reach is vast, and important too since wherever there is business activity there is strategizing. As a field, strategy has a long history from medieval and colonial times to today's developed and developing economies. This series offers a place for interesting and illuminating research including industry and corporate studies, strategizing in service industries, the arts, the public sector, and the new forms of Internet-based commerce. It also covers today's expanding gamut of analytic techniques.

Series Editor
J.-C. Spender
Kozminski
University

ISBN 978-1-009-24355-1

9 781009 243551 >

Cover image: irin-k/Shutterstock